A Politics of Identity

Kenneth R. Hoover

A Politics of Identity

Liberation and
the Natural Community

University of Illinois Press

URBANA CHICAGO LONDON

Library of Congress Cataloging in Publication Data

Hoover, Kenneth R. 1940–
  A politics of identity.

  Includes bibliographical references and index.
  1. Liberalism. I. Title.
HM276.H76   320.5'1   75-8797
ISBN 0-252-00436-1

for Judy

acknowledgments

My principal debt is to Murray Edelman, George Herbert Mead Professor of Political Science at the University of Wisconsin, both for his profound work in political science and his wise counsel. I am also beholden to Professor Erik Erikson for his encouragement.

Several generous readers and critics deserve to be cited (and exonerated): Booth Fowler, Donald Hanson, Suzanne Jacobitti, Henry Kariel, David Lorenzen, Mulford Q. Sibley, and Thomas Trautmann. Many hands have typed these pages, though I must especially acknowledge the assistance of Jean Shunk.

The Danforth Foundation provided vital support at an early stage. I am grateful to the National Science Foundation for a Faculty Fellowship, and the University of Wisconsin Department of Political Science and its chairman, Crawford Young, for facilities and assistance during the period of the grant. The National Endowment for the Humanities and the College of Wooster Faculty Development Fund assisted during the final writing.

I acknowledge with appreciation permission from The Hogarth Press, Ltd., to reproduce passages from *The Standard Edition of the Complete Psychological Works of Sigmund Freud,* revised and edited by James Strachey; from W. W. Norton and Co. to reproduce passages from *The Ego and The Id* and *An Autobiographical Study* by Sigmund Freud, and for quotations from the works of

Erik Erikson; and from the University of Chicago Press for quotations from *Mind, Self, and Society* by George Herbert Mead, copyright 1934 by The University of Chicago, 1962 by Charles W. Harris.

Throughout, I have been singularly fortunate to have had crucial support from good friends, interested colleagues, and, above all, an understanding family.

contents

chapter one

Introduction:
Liberalism and Liberation

A Political Prologue

Liberalism is in trouble. Both major political parties in the United States identify with liberalism's major achievement: the market society. Yet increasing numbers of people see the market system as oppressive rather than liberating. The market society is widely regarded as a device for perpetuating the advantages of the rich and powerful.[1] A series of new liberation ideologies arising from the anguish of groups kept subservient in the name of white, middle-

---

1. The generalizations reported here about the public assessment of liberal society are based on a review of public opinion polls over the last few years. A report which summarizes this development may be found in a Harris poll commissioned by the U.S. Senate Subcommittee on Intergovernmental Relations and described in *Newsweek*, Dec. 10, 1973, pp. 40–48. Of those polled, 76 percent (N = 1,596) agreed with the statement "The rich get richer and the poor get poorer" (up from 45 percent in 1966). Confidence in major institutions has declined markedly in six years. In response to the question "How has government changed your life?," 37 percent felt the federal government had made life *worse,* 34 percent no change, and 23 percent felt life had been improved; 45 percent felt the quality of life in general has worsened since 1963. While this level of disillusion has been sharpened by inflation, Watergate, and the energy crisis, these events themselves are symptoms of the muddle our political system is in.

class versions of liberalism hint at underlying elements of human nature which are frustrated and repressed in contemporary society.

If liberation is to mean that people should have control over their own lives, then liberalism can be said originally to have been a liberation ideology. The general idea that society should be constructed so each individual could get the best deal for himself in the marketplace while contracting with others for mutual defense of acquisitions was a distinct improvement over traditional hierarchic society. It is this aspiration for liberation which formed the symbolic attraction of liberalism to generations of humanitarians. It is the source of the liberal values of freedom, equality, and tolerance.

Yet there is a sharp distinction to be made between liberal values and traditional liberal solutions. Historically, private property, the market, and a socially sanctioned process of contract are the basis of liberal solutions to the human condition. It is these solutions which have run afoul of the inequities the market creates, the maldistribution of property and income, and the corruption of contract into a device whereby the rich control the government and its sanctions to the extent that contracts operate mostly for their benefit. There is a general feeling that community itself is being destroyed by an impersonal system.

The misfit of liberal solutions to liberal values suggests that there is something fundamentally wrong about the whole liberal analysis of human nature and its social correlates. Somewhere in the heart of liberal theory, there is a grave weakness.

The fault lines appear everywhere in the social upheaval of the sixties and seventies. The individualist values of early liberalism conflict with collectivist policies of the liberal welfare state. Each Congress, with liberals leading the pack, has delegated more and more power over the economy to the president, who, it seems clear, has sold the advantages of such power on the market of political contributions. The urge to increase regulation of the marketplace grows ostensibly out of a recognition of its failures in achieving social justice. Yet, at the same time, that regulation is guided, if at all, by only the most slipshod notions about what it is that will do any good. Even the bravest attempts at regulation in the name of the public interest become covers for special interest manipulators. The result has been a concentration of power made all the more potent by a tangle of policies which favor the well informed, the devious, and the clientele of smart lawyers. Meanwhile, welfare schemes succeed only minimally in handing out money to the poor and succeed much better in creating antagonism among taxpayers and clients alike. The effort to mobilize the poor to help solve their own problems in the Johnson administration led to a period of internal warfare between community action councils and city administrations which the latter, predictably, won in city after city. Model cities, the War on Poverty, Upward Bound, and a host of other programs were essentially junked by the Nixon administration on the general premise that everyone knows they didn't do any good. Whether or not they were effective, the political resolve which made these programs possible has evaporated under the hot wind of conservative clichés, for example, the "work ethic."

We are, in a sense, back to the 1950s in the area of social policy, with one major difference. Liberals are in disarray. Some still pursue the big government programs of the Johnson era and others have become skeptical. One perceptive liberal, who has been in the forefront of the struggle for some economy in our defense policies, Representative Les Aspin of Wisconsin, commented in an interview, "I don't see any great feeling among liberals that government can do everything. There's a feeling instead that [the government] just can't do it—that it will screw it up. . . . For anybody to try to launch a Great Society now—they just couldn't get very many votes." [2] Aspin's comment is significant in part because he is a Rhodes Scholar, a Ph.D in economics (M.I.T.), and a former aide to Secretary McNamara, the Council of Economic Advisers, and Senator Proxmire, as well as a widely respected politician.

2. "Liberal's View: Limit Government," an interview with Representative Les Aspin by Phil Haslanger, *Madison Capital Times*, Sept. 17, 1973, p. 21.

To the right of liberalism lies conservatism, with a miscellaneous repertoire of prescriptions which occasionally produce order, but seldom justice and sometimes neither. A conservative president and vice-president became tangled in their own transgressions of a Constitution they promised to strictly construe. Law and order, the cry of the Nixon administration, became an ironic reproach to its own machinations. To compound the irony, the Nixon administration presided over such an expansion of presidential economic power that it can almost be said America has achieved socialism without the difficulties of assuming direct control of the instruments of production. The president can now do almost anything he wants with the economic process. The Watergate scandals, particularly the extortion of campaign contributions from corporations, seem to suggest that we are or were on the verge of *national* socialism. Yet on the left, *democratic* socialists have yet to find that mixture of analysis and humanity which offers something other than the bureaucratized society so evident in the Soviet Union. As Chile demonstrates, middle-class liberalism allied with the military (and their international friends) still prevails even in the face of concerted efforts to alter dramatically the conditions of life.

The crucial battle in our society for an authentically humanitarian social creed proceeds only fitfully. The leaders and institutions which should be guiding the struggle are, often rightly, undermined by public suspicion, cynicism, and even hostility. The precipitate decline of public confidence in every major institution has been documented by public opinion polls.

Apart from the politics of the matter, the philosophic tradition of liberalism appears nearly bankrupt. The classic formulations of John Locke, John Stuart Mill, and Thomas Jefferson have not seen us through the complex political realities of the twentieth century. Neither "the greatest good for the greatest number" nor the concept of contract provides an adequate guide to the subtle interdependencies of life in contemporary society. Liberalism seems impotent in the face of racial conflict, revolution against an unresponsive political system, and the sophisticated challenges of planning for socioeconomic justice and ecological survival.[3]

Who Needs Political Philosophy?

What can a political philosopher accomplish in this situation? He or she dreams of finding in the ephemera of intellectual abstraction a vision of society which will inform a sound critique of social and political life. The philosopher is forever caught between the imprecision of a dream and ill-fitting evidence for a critique. Yet society, which relies heavily on dreams and myths, has need for sophisticated dreamers who also understand something of the rigors of practical analysis. The need is all the greater in a society unsure of its myths and deprived of some of its most impressive dreams.

This book looks again at humane values and tries to make sense of them in contemporary terms. The dream is to find an adequate definition of the public interest built on a sound view of human nature. The method is scientific pragmatism. The new trend of insight is psychological and psychoanalytic. The end object is a natural view of society built on liberty, equality, tolerance, and the other historic values of liberation ideologies. Such values are in trouble partly because there is neither a sensible modern defense of them nor a policy to guide their implementation. I am attempting here a defense and a policy, though I am all too aware that while society needs its dreamers, it has also learned the hard way to be wary of their creations.

A title like *A Politics of Identity: Liberation and the Natural*

3. See Theodore Lowi, *The End of Liberalism* (New York: Norton, 1969), and Robert Paul Wolff, *The Poverty of Liberalism* (Boston: Little, Brown, 1969). For a socialist critique of liberalism in the context of contemporary radicalism, see Christopher Lasch, *The Agony of the American Left* (New York: Knopf, 1969), esp. pp. 169–204. For an attempt to refurbish classical liberalism, see Donald Hanson, "What Is Living and What Is Dead in Liberalism?," a paper delivered at the 1970 American Political Science Association convention in Los Angeles.

Community requires at least a preliminary understanding of terms between the reader and the author. To begin near the end, the term *natural* has an immense history, yet I have in mind a simple usage. The capacities and potentialities of human nature are the keys to what a political community ought to look like. We want to find out what a natural political setting would be for human beings—in much the same sense as a wildlife specialist would want to know the appropriate environment for a species of animal. The problem is incredibly complex precisely because human beings are so *self* conscious. So, in addition to taking account of the material environment, we have to understand the psychological environment. I will use the term natural in order to indicate an aspiration toward that level of understanding. I do not mean by natural that which simply exists here in the present; rather I mean that which could exist if human beings were truly at home in their surroundings.

Liberation is linked to a natural view of the human environment almost by definition. Liberation refers to the creation of a genuinely human condition. Accordingly, liberation is both an inside and an outside phenomenon; it is personal as well as social. Liberation will come to mean here a process of human development in which the individual achieves a state of maturity and fullness of realization possible only in a certain kind of community.

The major term of the title of this book is *identity*. It is the phenomenon of human identity which provides the link between the problem of liberation and the specifications of a natural community. The scientific meaning of identity is to be found in the works of Erik Erikson, and I will explore that analysis in the last two chapters of the book. For now, it needs to be remarked that identity is a relationship, not a possession. In fact, it is a whole set of relationships between individual people and their surroundings in which they come to know themselves and to be known by others as individuals with particular repertories of skills, sensibilities, and responses. We will come to see that while the impulse toward identity formation is internally generated, the creation of a competent identity is an achievement both individual and communal.

While these sentences may appear as attempts at definitions, they are only intended as the foreshadows of meanings the reader can hope to expand as the discussion proceeds.

Since the angle of vision is significant for understanding what follows, a more specific summary of the plight of the traditional liberal is in order. Certain facts are apparent from the experience of contemporary social and political life. Endless competition dehumanizes people and destroys the environment and its resource base. Yet a little competition is demonstrably a good thing. Enforced cooperation shifts the focus of competition from goods and wealth to power and status. Yet a little enforced cooperation is a good thing. The structured representation of diverse interests at the seat of power institutionalizes the advantages of the rich and organized at the expense of the poor and disorganized. The poor and disorganized find it easier to turn to violence than to mobilize the "inputs" legitimized by the system. Yet some diversification of interests in the councils of the mighty is a good thing.

One species of liberal, the pluralist, argues that these dilemmas will resolve themselves if the processes of group pressure and persuasion are maintained and attended to. One suspects that trying to achieve harmony through organized contention is illusory. Yet these pluralists can point to a level, the most superficial level, of social science which reports what people in fact are doing in their political life. People seem to take behavioral cues from groups, to be poorly informed, to be susceptible to slick advertising in forming their voting decisions, and on the whole to be only peripherally concerned about politics. From this, it is easy to arrive at the prescription that politics should concentrate on group leaders and that politicians should not be unhappy about low citizen-participation—the "sleeping beast" theory. To the moralists who view with alarm the implied ethics of this position and the politics of the lowest common denominator, the liberal pluralists, now sounding more like seasoned English conservatives, answer that it isn't much, but it's the best that can be done. Moralists, idealists, and philosophically inclined liberals seem to be on weak ground in arguing with the pluralists. The studies appear to indicate that the voters aren't very smart, that conflicts of interest are endemic, and that corruption attends the concentration of power. Indeed, it does look as though conflict avoidance is the best that can be attempted by the political system. The reason for this weakness is that the only weapon available to the moral thinker is vision, and vision has been lost in our time. The intellectuals have overthrown the priests, who had a ready context for a vision in the theology of a godly creation. The intellectual in search of a vision usually turns, as Thomas Hobbes and John Locke did, to an analysis of human nature—a deeper and more profound exercise than an analysis of apparent behavior. The seventeenth, eighteenth, and nineteenth centuries are littered with tarnished visions of human nature which proved to be inaccurate, insufficient, or simply unbelievable. The twentieth century, with its graphic testimony to the brutality of civilized people and its scientific exploration of the aggressive aspects of human nature, has cast a pall over the vision seekers. The visionaries see the evil in humankind and they retreat. So the theorist hunts for some castle of words which will stand against the onslaught of discouraging empirical reality in human behavior.

It is much easier to describe the morass we are in than to point the way out. My approach reflects the twofold nature of the problem: the need for a method for finding the answers to questions about human nature, and the need to know what that method yields for present use. Both levels of argument are interdependent; we begin by looking at an initiative in political philosophy that shows us how *not* to proceed methodologically. I will look at an answer to the difficulties of liberalism which generated some suggestive solutions but which did not work for several instructive methodological reasons. Briefly put, it was the attempt to find in the abstractions of moral philosophy a sure ground for a revision of liberalism. Second, we need to go to the center of the matter: what method can we trust, and what does it tell us about human nature? This question is the key to understanding how society can go about arranging its institutions so as to liberate people. It is here that the science of psychology enters to guide us not by abstractions, but by adventuresome research into the basic elements that make people what they are.

Thus, the search for a vision takes the only method which makes sense in the twentieth century, the scientific empirical method, and I will look at the results not as final statements about that which shall ever be, but as clues to that old problem: the content of human nature. The behavior studied by social scientists is, after all, often localized to a small time period and a limited range of circumstances. Most behavioral studies are designed to contribute to short-range predictions about human behavior within a highly restricted range of variation in the contextual factors. By considering studies from more than one culture and from several dimensions of human behavior, it may be possible to glean some hints about the summary realities of human nature. The imaginations of such powerful thinkers as Sigmund Freud, G. H. Mead, B. F. Skinner, and Erik Erikson, among others, help span the gaps in hard knowledge.

So, my purpose is to analyze liberal values and to try to construct a more realistic defense of them. This will mean the modification of many liberal solutions. The task has dimensions which are specific to our contemporary political environment. As society becomes increasingly secular, the question of purpose behind life and culture becomes ever more urgent. A new philosophy of liberation must be both secular and satisfying as an explanation of purpose. At the same time, the accelerating power of the tools of collective action means that the task of justifying what we do is more immediate and significant than ever.

Given these dimensions, one could choose any of several starting points in the history of liberal thought. I have chosen a rather peculiar one: liberal idealism.[4] Peculiar because the title of the

4. T. H. Green's liberal idealist formulation will be used to establish the argument. For the sake of historical accuracy, it would be useful to include other idealists besides Green. The problem is that there are few

movement sounds quaint and antiquated and because the movement's founder, Thomas Hill Green, is a fairly obscure figure, especially in the popular recollection. Yet liberal idealism illustrates nicely the pitfalls of the moral philosophic approach to politics. At the same time there are some useful suggestions in liberal idealism. Green used a secular framework to discuss human purpose in a way that would integrate individual and community actions. Liberal idealism, in short, is a form of argument which directly attacks the central problem of liberalism: the reconciliation of self-interest with community.[5] It is through this relationship that the problems of racism, system responsiveness, and planning must be solved. We begin with T. H. Green only to get a foretaste of a set of values and ideas which can be more convincingly argued for on the basis of psychological theory.

Chapter Two sets out the meanings of liberal idealism, attacks the moral philosophic style in which they were developed, and demonstrates why, in the end, they are still important to contemporary problems.[6] At the same time, I will be looking at some

liberal idealists and most of them come after Green and diverge in orientation from Hobhouse on the left to Bosanquet on the right. A definitive obituary of liberal idealism is not within the scope of this project. The point here is to show the weakness of the method by which liberal idealism was initially formulated and to replace it with an argument based on a sounder method.

5. See Sheldon Wolin, *Politics and Vision* (Boston: Little, Brown, 1960), pp. 343–51. C. B. Macpherson focuses on the loss of liberal morality to "possessive individualism," based on Hobbes and Locke, which ties liberty to property and destroys community. It is this question of the essential content of self-interest which must be answered before community can be understood. My answer will differ from Macpherson's Marxist response, though I share his rejection of possessive individualism as a basis for liberalism. See C. B. Macpherson, *The Political Theory of Possessive Individualism* (New York: Oxford, 1962), esp. pp. 2–3.

6. The phrase *liberal idealism* requires definition since its meaning is tangled in a web of popular as well as technical meanings. The term *liberal* is fairly vague, but we will take it as a reference to a collection of values to be discussed in the text. The term *idealism* has a generally understood popular meaning and two technical philosophic meanings. In the popular sense, an idealistic philosophy is thought to refer to a rationale for

other secular arguments for liberalism only to show that they are part of the problems of contemporary thought rather than the solution. The familiar figures of Locke, Bentham, Mill, and Jefferson will enter briefly only to remind us of the unsolved problems in liberal theory.

From this starting point in the history of liberal thought, one goes on to what is new in this book: an investigation of the contributions to liberation, sometimes explicit and more often latent, in the ideas of Sigmund Freud, George Herbert Mead, B. F. Skinner, and Erik Erikson. The conclusion brings us to a new argument for liberation and some suggestions about applications to contemporary problems.

The psychological theorists who are presented here as political thinkers were not always deliberately playing that part. Freud, it is true, was reacting to some features of the prevailing political philosophy, but he did not attempt political philosophy in any systematic sense. George Herbert Mead appears chiefly as a pragmatic philosopher working out the implications of psychological

ignoring one's self-interest in the effort to do good for others. There is also a connotation of a certain optimism abut human nature. The philosophy developed here will support an ethic of human decency—though without conceding that human decency is counter to self-interest. The view of human nature which will emerge is optimistic though only in the sense that the potential of human nature is thought to be good—there are no promises of inevitable improvement in the affairs of humanity. As for its technical philosophic meanings, the term idealism is encountered in the study of *epistemology* (the theory of how humans learn) and in the speculation labeled *historiography* (the effort to find a directed meaning in the experience of history). In epistemology, the idealist position is that an individual's knowledge is the product of something more than data inputs from the senses. The empiricist or materialist, on the other hand, argues that knowledge is comprised of sense stimuli plus certain mechanical operations of the brain which compile and order impressions. For reasons that will become apparent, the discussion of epistemology is very important because it is really the key to whether people are totally the creatures of their environment or whether there is some margin of creativity in dealing with the stimuli which the senses transmit. As for the question of idealist historiography, of a Hegelian spirit directing the course of affairs, we shall be concerned only to reject such an explanation in favor of a more scientific noting of behavioral patterns and discontinuities.

investigations. B. F. Skinner confronts a considerable range of political theories in *Walden Two,* but he is, of course, principally celebrated for his insights into conditioning. Erik Erikson's essential task was the revision of Freudian insights and the reconciliation of psychoanalytic theory with problems of cultural change. The reason for reformulating the problem of liberation in terms of psychological evidence is to be found in the view of political theory which underlies this book. For the remainder of this chapter, I will describe the assumptions supporting that view. The origins of these assumptions are eclectic, and there will be no attempt to credit (or abuse) the sources.

The first set of assumptions has to do with the phenomenon of justification. It is assumed that people feel a need to justify what they do. The justifications which are generated as a result of this need are psychologically shaped by a more basic need—that of protecting one's own identity insofar as one's belief system is involved in it.

Second, it is assumed that while identity needs are basic to the justification process, there is also a kind of qualifying pressure in the creation of beliefs generated by the desire to come up with justifications which are culturally acceptable. What society regards as acceptable justification is evidenced by the philosophical *language of justification* peculiar to that culture. Natural law was the language of justification of the Middle Ages; scriptural interpretation served that purpose for other cultures; and references to the revelations of authority were used in yet other cultures and historical periods. In our recent past, moral philosophy attempted to fill this role. These languages of justification are arrived at for complex reasons, but they are not fanciful in that they codify the current state of accepted beliefs about human nature. The contents of these languages consist of myth, science, logic, and speculation.

Third, one function of political theory in all of this is both to illuminate the connections between values and the justifications available within the prevailing language and to inspect the justifications themselves for their consistency. These are the analytic functions of political theory. The principal normative function is to defend and attack value positions in terms of the prevailing language of justification, or its alternatives.

What this book is about, then, is the construction of a guide to liberation in terms of the prevailing language of justification in our time, that of science in general and psychology in particular. To say that science is the general language of justification in modern culture is not to say anything very controversial. The heavy emphasis on empirical demonstration, experiment, and quantification is evident in every area, from the natural and social sciences to television commercials which use the panoply of science to sell the most trivial products. The claim that psychology is the particular branch of science most relevant to the justification of political values may involve a bit more contention. Yet political theory is always built on assumptions about human nature. It is the discipline called psychology which, in our time, has systematized accepted beliefs about human nature.

Of Political Justification

It has already been noted that a justification for political values is constrained by the society's stock of knowledge and by the etiquette of its language of justification. This is not an absolute and necessary constraint of course, but rather a practical statement about the boundaries within which it is most effective to operate. In any event, a justification of political values must involve some general assessment of human nature—even if it amounts to a denial that there is a common human nature. It is at this point that experience enters. Unless we are to indulge in abstract model construction or in designing a theory for the gods instead of for ungodly humankind, it is fair to ask that these assumptions at least make some allusions to evidence about the dimensions of human behavior. Hobbes observed human nature in the laboratory of civil war. Machiavelli found support for his view of human nature in Roman history and in the fractured society of declining feudalism. Locke contemplated the soul of the English gentry for his impression of human nature. To turn in the twentieth century to the discipline of psychology is nothing innovative really, though it may appear that way because political theory can become a kind of self-contained enterprise indisposed to ecumenism.

The next step in justification is, it seems to me, to link a view of human nature logically to certain applications in the arena of value conflict. When Jefferson accepted the pantheist's belief in the "equality of man" based on the individuality and uniqueness of his creation by God, he had a clear basis for placing equality foremost among the values to be found in paragraph two of the Declaration of Independence. While we can legitimately ask for logical connections between a view of human nature and prescriptions for value ordering, the whole story of justification does not rest at this stage on logic alone. Once again, it is fitting to insist that some recourse to observation be involved.

Loosely speaking, the major premise of any justification must be a view of human nature, its minor premise an appreciation of the quirks in human behavior in relation to values, and the conclusion a proposition which is, in some respects, testable. The results of a justification, once taken to the point of application, will reflect on the accuracy of the major and minor premise. In a world of incomplete and imperfect empirical knowledge, logic provides a link between premises and conclusions while disciplined imagination spans the lapses in empirical knowledge.

It is hoped that the cutting and drying of assumptions resolves some of the questions which may occur to the reader. But an analysis of assumptions does not give a vivid enough picture of what the author feels political theory can do. Political theory is, beyond the analysis and dissection, an act of imagination. The title of Sheldon Wolin's essays on the history of political theory, *Politics and Vision,* is suggestive.

Political theory is like architecture in that the theorist is trying to see how political rather than aesthetic values can be realized through intellectual rather than physical materials in the environment. Architects can easily create leaky roofs in the process of fulfilling aesthetic values, as Frank Lloyd Wright did in abundance. Political theorists can create leaky justifications for political values by faulty fabrication of insights about human nature which the language of justification supports. Theoretic justifications must both "be right" in the sense of being consistent with the available insights, and they must "look right" in the sense of operating within the boundaries provided by a culture's language of justification.

So, political theory in this view is an act of imagination arising from the desire to transcend the limits of individual insight through logic and well-chosen evidence, and an act of discipline arising from the social and psychological dimensions of political justification in a given culture. In that sense, it is both normative and empirical. The aim is normative in that the hoped-for result is to provide a better justification for certain values than the unlettered could develop. But the constraints arise from empirical conditions—first, from the available stock of insights about human nature and, second, from the need to serve up the conclusions in a form which will meet the standards of intelligibility imposed by the accepted patterns of justification.

Accordingly, the unabashed aim of this book is normative: the justification of certain values. But the topics dealt with in the argument are empirical: the models of politics developed from nineteenth-century assumptions as contrasted with those developed through psychological research and theorizing. It is hoped that the conclusion will present a case for the possibility of employing elements of psychological evidence in favor of the values of liberation.

It may be that others who look at psychological evidence will find that it can be used to better advantage in the destruction of humane values. In fact, the author begins with the feeling that this is what psychological evidence has mostly been used for.

In any event, the purpose here is to join an argument. The working out of one's life situation is a dynamic process often characterized by contest and uncertainty. Well-justified arguments can be weapons in these skirmishes. The political theorist, in constructing a more acceptable defense for certain values, is developing a case for those values in a form which will enhance the prospects for their survival in the process of individual identity formation. A powerful justification can have the reflexive effect of encouraging espousal of certain values by providing a more accessible defense against justifications for competing values.

In other words, knowledge and power are, once in a while, connected.

chapter two

From Individualism
to Community

The puzzle of political philosophy is large and obviously intricate. Before one attempts to assemble the pieces in a new way, it is important to know both what a solution might look like and what will *not* work as a means to finding it. Political theory cannot be created *de novo* because it rests on the continuity of human experience. We are dealing here with the tattered remnants of a great tradition in the history of political thought: liberalism. Elements of that tradition are present in the catch phrases still widely used in our political culture: the public interest, the greatest good for the greatest number, the sanctity of contract, the dignity of man, etc. These phrases are the potent symbols of a vastly influential move to alter the pattern of human society.

Yet the relations between these phrases and the specifics of their meaning have become disjoint with contemporary experience. One often feels that the human urge to share is frustrated by a haze of nebulous concepts and conflicting arguments about what kinds of sharing will work and in what political framework. While the effort to find answers by sheer mental speculation, an example of which the reader will shortly encounter, remains attractive, we must realize the limits of that method. We will look briefly at two popular visions of liberalism to find how they went about simplifying the complexity of human behavior into formulations that might serve as a basis for a political system. A third vision of liberalism, less well known, will instruct us in the faults of the first two. It will also serve as a foil for a basic methodological argument: that the abstractions of moral philosophy do not contain answers. At the same time, we will come to see what the specific problems are that need to be solved.

Of Contracts, Pleasure, and Pain

Liberalism probably begins with a feeling that society can be a better place than the conservatives think. The term *liberal* is often found in the company of such terms as humanitarian, equitable, and reasonable. *Conservative,* by contrast, finds itself in the company of sterner words such as practical, realistic, and traditional. The problem for liberals in arguing with conservatives is that, when liberalism fails, conservative strictures seem to "work" as a way of restoring order (if not harmony) and stability (if not progress). Prisons are orderly and stable (though expensive).

The reverse relation does not hold: the failure of conservative prescriptions does not always lead to liberal successes. A badly fractured and alienated society may not immediately find in liberalism an answer to its problems. So the liberal is in the more difficult theoretical position. The liberal truly interested in liberation must have a clear and reasonable vision of something new; the conservative merely has to distill what is old. Conservatives have few visions beyond a sorrowful view of human nature. Liberals may have visions, but they often suffer uncertainty.

Liberalism in our political culture has, in the main, relied on two visions: contractualism and utilitarianism. Contractualism is the idea that individuals have certain interests which can be mutually protected through binding agreements. The major visionary here, of course, is John Locke (1632–1704). Though Locke alluded to natural rights and to God, there is nothing in the architecture of his ideas which requires a sympathy with religious beliefs. Locke's essential argument is that people have an interest in the property with which they have mixed their labor. By forming a *social* contract based on a mutual regard for private property, a society is created which serves that interest. By establishing a *political* contract in which government is organized for the purpose of attending to rules and regulations implied in property protection, a state is born. This is the foundation of the market society with its elaborate rules and institutions organized around the exchange of goods and services.

A critical understanding of Lockean contract must begin with an analysis of the general *idea* of contract as distinct from its *purpose*. Contract can be considered a metaphor for the mutuality of human endeavor. There is little evidence that societies began with the specific formulation of a contract, and less evidence that the contract is renewed in any direct way. True enough, participation in voting may be considered entry into a contractural relationship as may the benefits received from a school system or other state-supported services. However, the philosophic theory of contract is not satisfied unless individuals have a chance to freely enter into, or opt out of, a contract. It may be that individuals who do not like a specific political state can leave it. But we know too much about the conditioning of behavior to think that any individual has a free choice in any philosophically meaningful sense.

Still, the idea of contract has power as an analogy for an essential ingredient of human society: the exchange of rights and obligation between individuals. In order to rescue the idea of contract from its philosophic ambiguities, it is necessary, I will later argue, to translate it into a conception of inevitable social mutuality. Locke approaches this when he suggests that the social (as distinguished from the political) contract is irrevocable. The failure of Locke lies in the second component of his theory: the *purpose* of the contract as he saw it.

Locke argued that human nature places an individual's interest in the protection and enjoyment of private property: The exact content of his view of human nature is the subject of recurrent argument among scholars. The nub of the controversy is in what

Locke really meant by "property." Those critics who take a narrow view of the word property argue that government exists merely to protect rights and establish obligations relative to the ownership of assets and the conditions of physical labor. Those who take a wider view—that Locke meant to include all the efforts of an individual in his definition of property—may argue that society and government have a comprehensive responsibility to look after the "general welfare" of humankind.

I have nothing to contribute to settling the historical issue on this question. I'm not sure what Locke actually meant to say, but I am going to argue that he is wrong if he meant property narrowly, and misleading if he meant property broadly.

C. B. Macpherson has a telling comment about Locke's concentration on property when he points out that the "possessive individualism" which results from a property-based society is anything but liberating.[1] Riven by class warfare arising from the division of the population into landowners, land-workers, manufacturers, and laborers, such a society is likely to produce disproportionate power among classes. Inequities in *power* lead to the very situation which the contract was supposed to remedy: the inability of individuals to protect themselves from the depredations of others. What this tells us is not necessarily that the idea of contract is wrong, but that a society based on *property* contract and possessive individualism will revert to the conditions which generated the contract.

In a deeper sense, Macpherson suggests that Locke is wrong in isolating property as the primary interest of individuals. The working out of material self-interest inevitably leads to repression. The essence of a state built solely on property is the use of force to protect inequities of distribution. There is nothing positive or liberating about it unless one happens to be on top. Even then, life becomes a defensive proposition in which one patrols the borders of one's possessions with the assistance of the state.

1. See Macpherson's argument in *The Real World of Democracy* (Oxford: Clarendon Press, 1966).

Society becomes not a community but an agglomeration of isolated individuals.

The socialists in collectivizing all property are doing battle with Locke on his own terms and assumptions. The collectivization of property, in and of itself, doesn't seem to liberate anybody. The most it accomplishes is redistribution of goods on a more equal basis. This may be a good in itself, well worth having. But the experience of most socialist states is that material incentives of some kind are necessary in order to keep the society operating. The hierarchy of society begins to revolve a little less around personal property and a little more around power to control allocations of property and status at the collective (and even the international) level.

An exclusive social focus on property narrowly conceived is a circular proposition. A government built on this proposition merely rearranges the structure of property advantages without liberating anyone and usually with the attendant effect of reintroducing the divisions which society, whether liberal or socialist, was formed to overcome.

Those who read into Locke a broad definition of property bring him closer to a legitimately liberationist position. If the purpose of society is somehow to protect and enhance the whole effort of an individual's personal endeavors, we have something that sounds like liberation. The troubles are two: (1) why call this summation property? and (2) what does such a broad conception tell us that we need to know in prescribing the content of government action?

To call the summation of individual effort "property" is to give it a name which begs the question of society. Property is presumably that which one owns and wishes to defend. Society, on the other hand, is the expression of human mutuality and sharing, as well as of competition. So it may be worth quibbling over the term property as a useful label. Furthermore, the broad definition tells us what we are after without isolating what kinds of behavior need to be limited in order to ensure decent relations between individuals. We need a more specific, more operational, more precise theory than contractualism on which to build our liberation.

Utilitarianism, the second popular liberal vision, appears to provide a psychologically more sophisticated view of human nature than does Locke's possessive individualism. It is pleasure and pain which motivates individuals, not the pursuit of property. And utilitarianism purports to offer a calculus for the guidance of policy through the summarization of individual pleasures and pains. Jeremy Bentham (1748–1832) thought he was answering the need for a more scientific approach to public policy-making. At the same time, he was building on Locke's assumption that all knowledge arises from sensory experience.

The essence of utilitarianism is in the idea that human life is motivated by the "twin masters" of pleasure and pain. The minor assumption is that pleasure and pain are measurable— Bentham proposed that units of pleasure be termed "utiles." The early utilitarians believed that the calculation of utiles of pleasure and pain could best be done by the individual. Later utilitarians, principally John Stuart Mill (1806–73), modified this democratic view to argue that an elite in society might better be qualified to judge pleasure and pain.

There are two classic problems with utilitarianism. One is that nobody seems to be able to pin down the definition of pleasure (or pain) to anything which is operationally useful in discriminating between alternative courses of public action. Do people, in fact, have consistent judgments about pleasure and pain?

The second intrinsic problem is that there exists no workable calculus for measuring pleasure and pain which is sophisticated enough to take into account factors of intensity, duration, and comparability between persons. How do we assess a course of action which promotes mild pleasure for the majority and intense pain for the minority?

Aside from these inherent problems, there is a more profound objection which gets to the basic assumption that individuals may find their liberation by pursuing the pleasurable and avoiding the painful. In point of fact, people may insist on the painful occasionally. We can all think of examples of self-sacrifice which belie the utilitarian logic.

The attack on utilitarianism is the beginning point for a third division which has influenced liberalism, but which I have not classified among the two "popular" visions of liberalism. *Liberal idealism* is a vision which did have its influence on an important, though temporary, school of English political theorists. The essence of liberal idealism is that an individual is more than a sensor of utiles or an economizer of property—he or she is a thinking being who creates behavior through consciousness. It is this third vision which will occupy the remainder of this chapter because in it, I will argue, we find the shapes and forms from which a contemporary vision can be constructed.

The Ideal and the Real

The "common good," "the public interest," "positive freedom," "voluntarism," and "individual self-development" are all phrases loosely associated with liberal political philosophy. The currency given these political symbols is in part attributable to Thomas Hill Green. The difficulties of definition and application these terms have encountered in the twentieth century may also in part be laid at the door of Green's inadequacies as a moral philosopher and, indeed, of the weaknesses of the traditional style of moral philosophy. Because such terminology is important to liberalism, it is worth considering the system of ideas Green developed to link them together. And because of widespread demands for a more satisfactory philosophy of liberation, it is worth analyzing the problems which Green's enterprise leaves unresolved.

T. H. Green, tutor and fellow of Balliol College, Oxford, was a central figure in the intellectual world of high Victorian culture. That was a very special world. England achieved some kind of peak of historical development by the standards of the time. An adventurous and cultivated elite ruled an empire without and a civilized culture within. Oxford stood as a giant among universities and one of its truly imposing figures was Benjamin Jowett, master of Balliol College, tutor of political leaders, translator of Plato, and mentor of Thomas Hill Green (though he once dismissed Green's philosophical terminology as "fuliginous jargon"). Green's project in life was the revision of liberalism, the subject of his several substantial tomes.[2]

While we need not rehearse Green's ideas in detail, he is important because he stood at the confluence of several influential skeins of thought: English liberalism, German idealism, and evangelical Christianity. Compromisers are seldom great theorists. By bringing these traditions together, Green achieved a temporary reconciliation, but not a permanent solution as we shall see.

The first task is to establish some understanding of Green's argument, its origins, and its difficulties. This will lead us to a central point for future use: an examination of the methodology of T. H. Green as a moral philosopher. A second benefit of Green's ideas is in his incisive critique of Locke, Bentham, and Mill. These preliminaries will permit us to focus on the third clue Green provides for our purposes: the crucial concepts of *consciousness, positive liberty,* and the *common good.* Having gleaned what we can from these ideas, we may look for the flaw which cast doubt on the credibility of Green's idealism as a justification for liberal values.

T. H. Green, the Moral Philosopher

Modern philosophy began with Descartes's rationalist arguments concerning the nature of substance. These were aimed in part at supplying science with some bedrock concept on which all investigations could be built. This philosophic tradition arose not from

2. See his *Prolegomena to Ethics* (Oxford: University Press, 1890; hereafter *Prolegomena*) and *The Works of Thomas Hill Green* (London: Longmans, Green, and Co., 1885). The basic biographical source on T. H. Green is by R. L. Nettleship in the form of a *Memoir* in Vol. III of *The Works of Thomas Hill Green* (London: Longmans, Green, and Co., 1889), pp. xi–clxi. Melvin Richter's study is the most comprehensive: *The Politics of Conscience: T. H. Green and His Age* (Cambridge, Mass.:

a direct preoccupation with the explanation of human behavior, but rather from what philosophers thought was a prior enquiry, the basis of human existence and human knowledge. The classic battles of ontology need not concern us, but the philosophical method of these battles will.

Throughout the modern period philosophy has been an essentially introspective enterprise which developed its own rules, moves, and strategies much like those of chess. If a general principle was ennunciated, the task was to find a few convincing counter-examples. If a deduction was made from some grand principle, the job was to find a tautology or contradiction in the meaning of the terms. Another standard strategy for dealing with general principles was to outflank them through categorization. References to experience were confined largely to the searching out of counter-examples or to untested generalizations about what the common sense of the matter seemed to be or what the mass of people were supposed to be doing or thinking.

Behaviorism as a strategy of investigation begins, at least in theory, from the opposite direction. Rather than attempting by precise and exact definition of general mental concepts to know reality, behaviorism, to put it crudely, begins with the observable actions of individuals and tries to find patterns and discontinuities. Models are employed in the analysis of raw data, either consciously or unconsciously, and these models are, or should be, constantly tested against the data and revised accordingly.

It is the moral philosopher's dream to find that set of categories, axioms, and corollaries which would explain all of what is observable. The summit of this aspiration is to be found in the notion of the necessary causal relation—an abstraction drawn from overt

Harvard University Press, 1964). Richter explains Green's essential orientation in terms of his Christian evangelical convictions (see especially pp. 116–17). Richter's thesis is disputed by John Rodman in his very useful introduction to *The Political Theory of T. H. Green* (New York: Appleton-Century-Crofts, 1964), pp. 1–40. Rodman argues that Green is best seen as an exponent of German idealism as an answer to the dilemma posed by the discrediting of Christianity and the moral incapacities of scientific thinking (pp. 21–25).

behavior. The lesser goal was to so characterize and categorize human ideas that a justification could be developed which would support prescriptions for political, social, and moral life.

T. H. Green was of this philosophical tradition. He was, in addition, tied closely in upbringing, temperament, and surroundings to the Christian evangelical tradition in England. Green wanted to harness the power of philosophic insight to create a vision of a kind of good life which could be reached by ordinary individuals if they would but follow the cues and hints provided in their daily intercourse with the world. That is, he set out to develop a model of human consciousness, an abstract model derived from general propositions about people in their social milieu, which could be seen by inference to relate to the common aspirations of humankind. If these inferences could be accepted as valid, so also could Green's prescriptions for the best modes of political organization and state action. This was Green's methodology.

T. H. Green's formal philosophic starting point was a critique of the whole tradition of British empiricism and the utilitarianism which he felt was its direct descendant. A major part of Green's collected works consists of critiques of Locke, Berkeley, Hume, Mill, Spencer, and Lewes. It would be tedious and unnecessary to review all of these critiques. There were two central arguments which Green deployed against previous liberal philosophy. The first was a critique of utilitarian pleasure-pain assumptions on the ground that they could not satisfactorily explain important aspects of human conduct. The second argument was an attack on the theory of knowledge which supported empiricism.

In his commentary on the pleasure-pain principle, Green asserted that human behavior cannot be explained without reference to abstract goals and ends. He notes, in an analysis of Locke's definitions of happiness, that reference is made to the "greatest sum of pleasure" and "pleasure in general," both abstractions of a very high order.[3] Green's contention is that a distinction needs to

3. Green, *Prolegomena,* p. 398. See also *Works,* Vol. I, p. 307.

be made between the random pursuit of discrete pleasures and the quest for a general state of pleasure. The former, says Green, is really what utilitarianism is based on, and it does not explain many self-sacrificing acts of human behavior. These acts demonstrate that the study of human behavior must reveal a pursuit of some abstractly defined general good for the self. The self is capable of innovation and can direct its efforts toward the improvement of itself and others. Out of this, Green goes on to show, comes the idea of a highest good defined apart from discrete pleasures.[4]

Furthermore, according to Green, the pursuit of particular pleasures always winds up in self-defeat occasioned by excessive indulgence with attendant effects of satiation, boredom, and the quest for new pleasures. It is more realistic to see that a person seeks a state of satisfaction to which certain pleasures and even certain pains may contribute.[5] The problem is ignorance of precisely what this state of satisfaction entails. Individuals grope for a state of satisfaction through the pursuit of specific pleasures. These discrete pleasures are not viewed as ends in themselves; indeed, they cannot be that. Rather, they are thought to be elements of that abstract state of satisfaction. Sensualism is a preoccupation with the temporary, when it is the eternal that should be pursued.[6]

The second level of his critique of liberalism goes closer to the heart of the matter. Locke set the basis for three centuries of liberal thought in a revolutionary concept of the way humans learn about the world. Prior to his time, it was generally accepted that people were born with ideas about the world pre-formed in their minds. Theologians attributed this to divine will.

Locke and his utilitarian heirs, Bentham and Mill, agreed that individuals are born with a "blank tablet" for a mind. As sensory experience writes on the tablet, people build up learning about the

4. Green, *Prolegomena,* pp. 237, 391.
5. Green, *Prolegomena,* pp. 91, 226; *Works,* Vol. I, pp. 304–16, *Works,* Vol. 3, p. 226.
6. Green, Prolegomena, p. 414; *Works,* Vol. 1, pp. 305–10.

nature of life. Thus, experience is the center of learning, and *empiricism* is the name given this theory of knowledge. Green's theory of knowledge is derived from the Germans Kant and Hegel, which places Green in direct opposition to the English empiricist tradition. Green's position is no surprise: he argued that human knowledge simply could not be explained as the accumulation of sense impressions, no matter how fancy the apparatus for combining and abstracting sense impressions is deemed to be. The mechanical processes of absorbing sense impressions cannot make up "the man capable of knowledge." People must be something more than simply sensors.[7]

But what is it in humans that is separate from their sense impressions? The answer is *consciousness*. In Green's lexicon consciousness implies the capacity to move beyond what *is* to what *might be*. It is crucial to an understanding of this powerful concept to know the route by which he arrived at it.

Green's "theodicy," as Melvin Richter terms it in his study of him, demanded that there be some overarching purpose in human life beyond sensory experience and above the mundane level of pleasure and pain. Green posits the nebulous category *consciousness* and uses it to explain why human beings aspire not to discrete pleasures but to a state of satisfaction, and why an individual is more than a simple collector of impressions. The human being is conscious, which means that individuals move beyond the immediate experience of pleasure and pain to anticipate a future state of being. One can select, reorder, and interpret sense impressions into knowledge. While these propositions about the content of consciousness have the form of arguments from empirical analysis, Green never pretended to have done any actual experimentation on human behavior. He does evoke general observations to make his arguments plausible on the empirical level, but it is far more likely

---

7. Green, *Prolegomena,* p. 86. See also Richter, *Politics of Conscience,* pp. 178–79, 186. Regarding Locke, see Green, *Works,* Vol. 1, p. 62; regarding Hume, Vol. 1, p. 176, and Vol. 3, "Popular Philosophy in Its Relation to Life," pp. 92–125; and regarding Spencer and Lewes, Vol. 1, pp. 375–76, 419, 455–56, 516.

that Green's observations on these points were called up to defend what was a metaphysical necessity in his argument: that abstract ideas be established as the central force in human behavior.

Of the actual content of consciousness, Green had little to say that was not derived from basic axioms of metaphysical speculation and imputed to the human mind. However, at this point it is important to pin down the moves Green made in arguing from *a critique of empiricism* to an *idealist theory of human purpose.*

The argument progresses as follows:

1. Knowledge consists of the *relationships* between sense impressions, not the impressions themselves. Therefore, there exists a set of relations independent of impressions.

2. These relations of knowledge are true independently of individual knowledge of them. (The appropriate example would be the axioms of mathematics.)

3. If there is such knowledge, then there must be an eternal set of relations or, by a kind of conceptual transmutation, an *eternal consciousness* since consciousness is essentially knowledge.

4. Knowledge is therefore the *individual realization* of this eternal consciousness—though the act of realization for each individual is unique, nondetermined, and thus a free manifestation of the individual.[8]

Green's arguments here are an interesting combination of Kant, Hegel, and Aristotle.[9] Without untangling the history of it all, it is possible to cite a leap in his argument from a theory of knowledge to a theory of the purpose of human existence. It is one thing to

8. The steps in this argument may be seen in Green, *Prolegomena*, pp. 22–23, 72–86; *Works*, Vol. 3, p. 4. See also Richter, *Politics of Conscience*, pp. 174–75, and Green, *Works*, Vol. 3, p. 53.

9. See Aristotle, *Nicomachean Ethics*, W. D. Ross edition (London: Oxford University Press, 1915), Bk. 6, Ch. 7, and Green, *Works*, Vol. 3, pp. 85–86. See also Immanuel Kant, *Critique of Pure Reason* (New York: St. Martin's, 1929), Introduction, pp. 41–62, and Green, *Lectures on the Principles of Political Obligation* (Ann Arbor: University of Michigan Press, 1967), p. 9. See also G. W. F. Hegel, *Reason in History: A General Introduction to the Philosophy of History* (New York: Bobbs Merrill, 1953), Ch. 2, "Reason as the Basis of History," pp. 11–19, and Green, *Works*, Vol. 3, p. 146.

argue that there is more to knowledge than the classification of sense impressions, and quite another to suggest that there is an ultimate consciousness which contains all the true relations of knowledge.

Green may be right in claiming that the mind prestructures discrete physical sensations into perceptions which are related to form knowledge, and quite wrong in claiming that there is an eternal consciousness in which all individuals participate. What were once thought to be "true relations," e.g. a straight line is the shortest distance between two points, are now seen to be either false (as is the case with the example after Einstein) or the product of the terms employed.[10]

Green's "leap" is essentially an act of faith that reason is the underivable principle behind all human consciousness. Reason is the human genius, and thus the expression of the divine. However much Green would like us to be persuaded that this dogmatic proposition is the result of logical demonstration from an analysis of knowledge, we must recognize that it is simply a postulate.[11]

Some critics might wish to say that whatever Green hangs on this leap must be considered interesting, but undemonstrated and therefore unacceptable as the basis for a normative philosophy. According to the formal canons of philosophy, this is the correct conclusion. However, our inquiry need not be limited to the

10. For a summary of the criticism of Green by Russell and Moore, see Richter, *Politics of Conscience*, pp. 188–89.
11. Green, *Works*, Vol. 3, *Memoir*, pp. xxxviii–ix, lxxi. See also Richter, *Politics of Conscience*, pp. 181, 214–15, 229. Reason was for Green not only the underivable principle behind human consciousness, it was also the *summum bonum* of human activity. Green was at times conscious that he could not really justify such a goal apart from a rather murky relationship to epistemology: "If we ask for a reason why we should pursue this end [rationality], there is none to be given but that it is rational to do so, that reason bids it, that the pursuit is the effort of the self-conscious or rational soul after its own perfection. It is reasonable to desire it because it is reasonably to be desired. Those who like to do so may make merry over the tautology. Those who understand how it arises—from the fact, namely, that reason gives its own end, that the self-conscious spirit of man presents its own perfection to itself as the intrinsically desirable—will not be moved by the mirth." *Prolegomena*, p. 411.

methodology of formal philosophy. Green was expressing a tradition of speculation that human behavior is informed by more than mechanical responses to sense stimuli. There is enough human behavior which in inexplicable in terms of what Green called "naturalism" that it is worth pursuing his concept of consciousness to see what content he does ascribe to it and how he builds a political philosophy on it. That Green posited his central concept rather than deriving it from observation does not preclude the possibility that it has explanatory utility. Furthermore, an understanding of Green illuminates a valuable vision of liberalism—one which affected behavior in political movements. The justification for converting such a vision into normative philosophy must, however, remain in doubt.

Green's concept of consciousness relies heavily on Hegelian notions of a spiritual principle in the universe as well as on Aristotelian ideas of human potential. Green thought that human striving is intelligible as activity in the face of a contradiction between what one is and what one could be. The recognition of that dialectical contradiction is the distinguishing feature of the human mind. There is a world of potential good which one can realize in specific actions. Green sets up the consciousness of a potentially better future as something like the Hegelian Idea acting in each individual life. As will be noted later, his conception of the "eternal consciousness" is a good deal less grand than Hegel's "Idea."

Aristotle's influence on Green is readily apparent both in Green's use of the concept of potential and in Green's celebration of the preeminence of the rational in the mind. While human nature is not unalloyed rationalism, it is the rational impulse which is responsible both for human knowledge and the social instinct.[12]

As for human desires which seem irrational, Green has an interesting argument. Desires are actually expressions of a striving for a better state of general satisfaction. As such, desires are linked in "a system, connected by memory and anticipation, in

12. Green, *Works,* Vol. 3, *Memoir,* p. lxxi; see also Aristotle, *The Politics,* Barker translation (New York: Oxford University Press, 1962), p. 317.

which each is qualified by the rest." [13] This *system* of desires is expressive of the human moral urge to better oneself. Specific impulses of desires can be destructive, and the function of reason is to bring the whole system of desires into harmony with the "higher interest" of the self. Nature itself is a reflection of this same consciousness, and its laws may be brought into harmony with human development—a pantheistic twist to Green's theology which separated him from the Christian orthodoxies of his time.

The central problem of human existence is that one cannot have direct knowledge of eternal consciousness. The individual cannot even see very far into the consequences of his or her acts. But the very fact of being related through one's own potentiality to the ultimate development of humankind is enough to provide a beginning point for a system of morality. Green presents human consciousness essentially as a disposition to know more and to achieve new heights of self-development.

While it is true that self-development is, in a sense, further immersion in the eternal consciousness, each individual is free because the successive acts of appropriating the eternal consciousness are products of the individual's own volition. This is the meaning of *will* in Green's conception—and it is arrived at through the same process of deduction from a priori assumptions as is consciousness. In a more sophisticated sense, a person is determined in that which might be achieved, but he or she cannot know in advance the content of that determination since the ultimate form of consciousness is unknowable.

The relation of all this to political philosophy is that the important liberal idealist concept of a *common good* enters through Green's analysis of consciousness. The "permanent well-being" that people desire necessarily involves the individual in the well-being of others. "Some sort of community, founded on such unity of self-consciousness, on such capacity for a common idea of permanent good, must be presupposed in any groupings of men from which the society that we know can have been developed," Green

13. Green, *Prolegomena,* p. 133.

wrote.[14] The destiny of humankind is a common destiny, and this is the message of reason, the master of consciousness. Green's evidence here is that there are observable efforts by individuals to better themselves collectively which are explicable in no other way. The standard of morality becomes the end toward which an act is directed: if it be toward the improvement of one's character and that of others, it is moral because this is the *terminus ad quem* of humankind and is therefore the only action of lasting benefit. If the object of an act is merely the appropriation of some thing or transitory pleasure, it is not moral and must be temporary in its gratification. Green outflanked utilitarianism by defining ultimate happiness as the realization of successive states of improved consciousness.

Throughout, Green is really arguing from the *idea* of good to the *actuality* of a preeminent human impulse toward good. One can appreciate the objection of Arthur Bentley when he commented, "We must deal with felt facts and with thought facts, but not with feeling as reality or with thought as truth." [15]

Students of nineteenth-century thought will recognize in Green's incurable optimism the familiar nineteenth-century credo of progress. Green sees history as a continuous development of institutions and practices which elevate human activity from its temporary diversions toward the edifice of common consciousness and moral improvement. The belief in progress was in no small part a reflection of evangelical Christianity as Green knew and believed in it. Green's enterprise was actually to appropriate such Christian concepts as individual dignity and redeemability for a new philosophy based on neo-Hegelian idealism.

The concept which undergoes the most interesting transformation in this process of appropriation is that of evil. Green sees no independent evil. The perfectly reasonable individual would never do evil. Evil, for Green, is a judgmental mistake. Evil is not a conscious rejection of the good in that, if its consequences were

14. *Ibid.*, p. 212; see also p. 279.
15. Arthur Bentley, *The Process of Government* (Cambridge, Mass.: Harvard University Press, 1967), p. 172.

known to the miscreant, the person would not do it. Neither is the doing of evil an unmitigated disaster, because the consequences of it are often the instrument of rectification. Habit and lack of energy to do the perceptual work involved in avoiding evil must be overcome by the force of reason and the desire to do better.[16] Thus, society has a role in both removing obstacles to the realization of right reason and, at the same time, protecting its members from the consequences of other people's inadequacies as moral reasoners. The great advantage of Green's doctrine of evil is that it places the burden of wrong choices on humankind itself while dispensing with some of the more fanciful mythology in the Christian tradition.

The preceding disgression on the concept of evil is designed partly to show how Green answers the obvious rejoinder to his optimism and partly to illustrate how his system of idealist definitions permits him to avoid a careful examination of human behavior.

16. Green, *Works,* Vol. 3, *Memoir,* p. 249 ff. For Christians evil is a kind of separate strain in the world, always presenting itself as an option for the free choice of persons. It is perhaps too strong to characterize the classic Christian position by positing evil as a totally independent force. In order to square with fundamental Christian tenets of an all-powerful God, it must be true that evil is in some way caused by God (as in the myth of the fall of Satan). Though both the Satan myth and the Adam and Eve myth shift the blame for the institution of evil onto humanity or to pride existing in an angel who was less than God, the fact remains that God is the creator of all. At any rate, evil is envisioned as operating independently, as the rich literature on the devil testifies. The paradox of an omnipotent God and an independent evil has never been solved by Christianity. In this century particularly, that paradox appears to be the most corrosive solvent of the traditional edifice of theology. For T. H. Green, the matter of evil poses a similar paradox, but he resolves it in a different way. If eternal conciousness is realizing itself through human actions and institutions, then how can there be evil? Green answers by elaborating on the classic Socratic position that knowledge is virtue, and evil is to be seen merely as ignorance. There is no such thing as an evil motive. There is simply the desire at every moment to go beyond present limits on one's own self-realization toward some greater development of one's potential. This desire can lead into blind alleys, as Green guarantees the voluptuary will find out. Drinking, womanizing, and vices of all sorts, when perceived as paths to an ultimate state of pleasure, will turn out to be inherently limited. The lack of knowledge or an adequate reasoning process leads us into these blind alleys.

We have been concentrating on T. H. Green's use of the methodology of moral philosophy to illuminate such concepts as consciousness and evil while criticizing the formulations of utilitarians. The a priori nature of his assumptions and the unwarranted leap from a theory of knowledge to a theory of purpose have been examined. One task remains for this chapter: the presentation of Green's model of politics.

The Liberal Idealist Model of Politics

The explication of Green's liberal idealist model of politics is perhaps best organized by the major concepts involved: moral duty, the common good and the public interest, the basis of rights, obligation, and positive liberty. The concepts, some of which will be revitalized in later chapters, originate in Green's metaphysics. They are the parts of his political philosophy which theorists must take as the application of liberal idealism to the real problems of normative inquiry.

"My *duty* is to be interested positively in my neighbour's wellbeing. And it is important to understand that, while the enforcement of obligations is possible, that of moral duties is impossible." [17] This is Green's own summary of his concept of moral duty. The justification for it is derived from the idealist assumption that the good of one individual cannot be conceived apart from the good of others. There is no such thing as a complete human being who is antisocial. Green here affirms the classic Greek vision of the social person: self-development not only of an inner set of abilities, but of a relationship to others as ends in themselves.

The performance of duty is an instrument of self-realization. Every individual is an artisan in the development of the eternal consciousness. At the same time, self-realization is intrinsically a voluntary process. No one can do it for someone else. As self-realization is undertaken through an act of will by the individual, so is moral duty.

17. Green, *Principles of Political Obligation,* p. 246.

There are such things as obligations (to be discussed later), but the performance of duty is made moral by its voluntary character. Habit can reinforce the performance of duty and this is to be encouraged. Moral duties are "duties to act from certain dispositions and with certain motives, and these cannot be enforced." [18] The function of government, Green proclaims, is to make it as easy as possible for people to carry out voluntary acts of moral duty.

It is obvious that Green's conception of moral duty relies heavily on a Hegelian framework. The purpose of individual life is to realize the eternal consciousness in whatever small way one can. The general maxim which guides the individual is that self-realization is interdependent with the well-being of others. The real job is not to lose sight of that end. Once one is convinced of the logic of it, the performance of duty will be relatively easy.

Implicit in Green's concept of moral duty is the idea of *the common good* or the public interest, one of the most influential notions of liberal idealism. As Richter points out, in liberal idealist philosophy, "society is based, not on contract or utility, but upon the spontaneous recognition by persons of other persons as ends in themselves and the further recognition that the interests of those others is involved with their own interest." [19] Green allows

18. *Ibid.*, pp. 34, 39–40. See also *Prolegomena*, pp. 218–21.

19. Richter, *Politics of Conscience*, pp. 232–33. In fact, the preceding examination of Green's political thought reveals broader parallels between the form of argument used in moral idealism, natural law, and Jeffersonian deism. The idea of self-development through a common *telos* is as old as Plato, but it is also congruent with the natural-law argument that each individual has a natural place in society. Jefferson, with his view of God as the master-builder, and the individual as the unique expression of the various facets of his design, is presenting a justification not unlike Green's. Natural-law proponents have historically argued that the dignity of humankind stems from participation in the development of nature. (The view of Jefferson is based on Daniel Boorstin, *The Lost World of Thomas Jefferson* (Boston: Beacon, 1948), and on Carl Becker, *The Declaration of Independence: A Study in the History of Political Ideas* (New York: Knopf, 1942).) Arnold Brecht, in his history of contemporary political theory, lists the development of moral idealism as the third in a long series of revivals of natural law—a revival eclipsed in about 1900 by scientific

that there may be a stage in the early history of a people when the struggle for subsistence preempts the consciousness of a common good, but, in characteristic nineteenth-century fashion history is progress and there always arises an effort toward common betterment.

The laws of any society are the instruments of advancing the common good. The law may on occasion be out of tune with the common good, and Green cites conditions when the discrepancy becomes sufficiently apparent for the justification of civil disobedience. But the common good is nearly always served by the general habit of obedience to the law.[20] The very idea that there is a common good is radical. A controversial idea with a history as long as recorded thought, the "common good" or the "public interest" has been the cry of liberal reformers all over the world. Green's discussion of the idea was particularly influential because of the long reign of individualism in English thought. The notion was extended in the works of L. T. Hobhouse, whose analogy for the state was that of an interdependent organism which should be directed toward its own common advancement.[21] Hobhouse, as well as Green before him, was sensitive to the failure of utilitarian liberalism which stimulated competition to the extent that com-

value relativism only to be superseded by another revival in the form of a revolt against relativism, which he dates from 1920 to the present (Brecht, *Political Theory,* Princeton, N.J.: Princeton University Press, 1959), pp. 140–41). Whatever the merits in Brecht's classification, the similarities in these arguments is not surprising since Green was, as previously indicated, appropriating the concepts of Christianity for an essentially atheological form of idealism. What is significant is that the defense of liberal values so clearly involves reference to some form of abstraction from experience. The "eternal consciousness" of moral idealism, the Jeffersonian masterbuilder, and the Newtonian God of the natural-law theorists are all teleological abstractions in terms of which central values are justified. However, my thesis is that in a secular society, it is essential that the question of the designs attributable to human nature be discussed in a more scientifically defensible manner.

20. Green, *Principles of Political Obligation,* pp. 150–51.

21. Leonard Trelawney Hobhouse, *Liberalism* (New York: Oxford University Press, 1964), from the Introduction by Alan Grimes, p. 7.

munity was destroyed. The malleability of the concept reflects its origins in abstractions about man's ultimate purpose.

The difficulty in the notion can be seen in Aristotle's comment that "men journey together with a view to some particular advantage, and to provide something that they need for the purposes of life. . . ." [22] Which is it? Particular advantage or the purposes of life that bind men? Of course both do, and liberal idealism tries to reconcile the two. Green's definitions permit him to say that there is no "particular advantage" apart from the common good properly understood. But a skeptical Arthur Bentley can dismiss such formulations generally as " 'talk,' and at that not even talk that goes to the point, but talk at long range, talk that colors, that lights up, that pleases aesthetically, that stimulates, but that for the purposes of close investigation is negligible except as its exact meaning at any given time and place may be definitely established." [23]

Yet such talk can have great power as the symbol of reform movements. Giovanni Sartori, speaking as a liberal in the bitter atmosphere of Italian politics, reminds us that "Politics without adjectives, or pure politics, is based at one time or another on nationalism, racialism, imperialism, or simply patriotism," and these are names for versions of the "common good." [24]

Green does give some content to the idea of the common good in the form of his concept of *positive freedom,* which I will examine more closely after considering his view of rights and obligation.

Idealists are on the strongest ground when they argue from the obvious fact of man's social nature to the idea of a common good. Green says that this ability of man to understand his relationship to others is the foundation of *rights.* Rights are conventions which facilitate the fuller realization of human nature. Rights are neither social artifice nor are they natural in the classic sense that they

22. Aristotle, *Nicomachean Ethics*, p. 541, lines 8–15, Section 1160a.
23. Bentley, *The Process of Government*, p. 117.
24. Giovanni Sartori, *Democratic Theory* (Detroit: Wayne State University Press, 1962), p. 34.

precede society. Rights are part of the idealist definition of man; ". . . they arise out of, and are necessary for the fulfillment of, a moral capacity without which a man would not be a man." [25]

The state is a collection of people who mutually recognize that such rights exist as a complement to human nature. The institution of the state, to be moral, must protect and extend those rights. So the chain of interlocking concepts culminates in *the state:* from consciousness to duty to common good to rights to the state. And, as might be expected, the concept of *obligation* is the next link in the chain.

Since the state is the protector of rights essential to any individual's self-development, the basis of obligation is clear. One must of course be obligated to that which is so intimately tied to one's very humanity. A person is obligated to the state in somewhat the same way as he is obligated to his parents for bringing him into the world. The realization of the eternal consciousness depends on the establishment of a just state. Without a just state, people cannot be secure in those circumstances which will lead to their own most expeditious development. Obligation is thus derived, as are Green's other major concepts, from this theory of purpose.[26]

While the state is a necessary condition for the process of self-realization and therefore deserving of obedience, so also is a certain kind of individual freedom necessary. Perhaps the most celebrated of the concepts fostered by liberal idealism is that of *positive liberty*.

The phrase arises from a rejection of the utilitarian concept of freedom—the freedom to be left alone in the competitive race for one's values. The scandal of nineteenth-century English liberalism was the abuses to its fundamental values of equality and individual autonomy which were perpetrated under the weal of a *laissez-faire* definition of liberty.

Green redefined liberty as "the maximum of power for all

25. Green, *Principles of Political Obligation,* p. 47; *Works,* Vol. 3, *Memoir,* p. cl; Adam Ulam, *Philosophical Foundations of English Socialism* (New York: Octagon, 1964), p. 34.

26. Green, *Prolegomena,* pp. 352–53; see also *Obligation,* pp. 122, 137.

members of human society alike to make the best of themselves. . . ." [27] The significant element here is the introduction of the term *power* into the definition of the term *freedom*. An individual without the tools to make his or her way in the world is not free. The power of the state must be deployed to liberate the individual's own resources for moral activity. The shift from the idea of liberty as freedom *from* state action to liberty as the aim of positive state action on behalf of individuals is powerful indeed. In the 1960s some fundamental civil rights laws were formulated on this same premise. The state becomes the active partner of the oppressed in preventing discriminatory action by restaurant owners, real estate agents, and voting registrars.

In the process of working out the meaning of positive freedom, Green came as close as he ever would to providing a practical program for liberal idealism. A major target was drink. Green was a significant figure in the temperance movement. He felt the state is justified in removing the temptation to drink, a temptation which leads to the abnegation of the moral faculty in individuals. A person's freedom to drink is a negative freedom in that it damages moral fibre and may lead to nearly irreversible addiction and the accompanying degradation. Sober people, these Victorians!

A more convincing application of his philosophy of positive freedom was to the problem of contracts. The Irish Land Act of 1870 was a great victory in the transition from the utilitarian position that the state should enforce any contract made between adults to the idealist position that there are some contracts which "from

27. Green, *The Political Theory*, p. 53. Actually, the concept of positive liberty is anticipated in John Stuart Mill's revision of utilitarianism: "In a world in which there is so much to interest, so much to enjoy, and so much also to correct and improve, everyone who has this moderate amount of moral and intellectual requisites is capable of an existence which may be called enviable; and unless such a person, through bad laws, or subjection to the will of others, is denied the liberty to use the sources of happiness within his reach, he will not fail to find this enviable existence, if he escapes the positive evils of life, the great source of physical and mental suffering. . . ." *Utilitarianism*, reprinted in *The Utilitarians* (Garden City, N.Y.: Doubleday, 1961), pp. 415–16. See also Matthew Arnold, *Culture and Anarchy* (Cambridge University Press, 1966), pp. 62–63.

the helplessness of one of the parties to them, instead of being a security for freedom, become an instrument of disguised oppression." [28] Once again the state is seen to be using its power to ensure conditions which facilitate moral improvement.

Other schemes, such as compulsory school attendance, are justified by the same logic. It is through the concept of positive freedom that the idea of the public interest is most clearly expressed. The difficulty is that decisions as to which freedoms are positive and which are negative may as likely be based on ensuring privilege for the few as on any behaviorally tested theorems. On the other hand, that form of government which ostensibly guarantees the most procedural liberty, namely democracy, may not through its processes yield an intelligent classification of freedoms. Leaving people free to do whatever they want may yield repression rather than liberation. Hobhouse was more realistic on this point than Green. Green thought that as a matter of practical fact, most people simply accept the institution of government and that a few people of good intentions shape them to the common benefit. Hobhouse saw that the majority might not follow what is best for the community.[29] The paradox which results is summed up by Herman Finer: "Here is the everlasting difficulty of government which wishes to remain free: to admit the right and the necessity of spontaneous development, and yet to find the norms which shall provide regulation without suppression." [30]

The power of symbols and what Sartori calls the *deontology* of democracy can be made to give substance to such an idea as positive freedom, but the practical arrangements for distributing power so as to maximize such a concept require widespread adherence to an explanation of what is positive and what is negative. The failure of such a consensus yields the kind of modern state char-

28. Green, *The Political Theory,* pp. 67–68.
29. Hobhouse, *Liberalism,* pp. 41–42, Ulam, *Philosophical Foundations,* p. 62; cf. Bentham on "plans" in *The Handbook of Political Fallacies* (New York: Harper, 1962), p. 201.
30. Herman Finer, *Theory and Practice of Modern Government* (New York: Holt, Rinehart, Winston, 1949), p. 96. Finer's own maxim may be found on p. 77.

acterized by a constitution which, in the words of Murray Edelman, becomes ". . . the concise and hallowed expression of man's complex and ambivalent attitude toward others: his wish to aggrandize his goods and powers at the expense of others; his fears that he may suffer from powerful positions of others and from their predations; his seeking for an encompassing principle that will introduce stability and predictability into this explosive clash of interests." [31] Green retained a faith in "leveling" and in the enlightenment of the masses which was a brave affirmation of his vision, however risky it was in terms of political realities.

One cannot help but admire the act of faith of Thomas Hill Green in maintaining that the content of morality arises from the general articulation of an indefinite consciousness that there is something that could be other than what is. This articulation takes place and progresses when rights are secured and the state operates to provide the best conditions.

Green's model of politics in relation to the state is almost purely abstract. The only convincing reference to experience is the observation that utilitarianism cannot explain certain kinds of valorous conduct. Each concept builds on the preceding one, and all are founded on Green's assumptions about the eternal consciousness. It is easy to dismiss such a model as having little worth because of its very abstractness as well as its logical failures. However, the value problems Green addresses are classic, and his secular community-oriented approach is one which is not wholly irrelevant in an agnostic, if not atheistic, age.

Conclusion

It can be said that Green's idea of an eternal consciousness is a rather spare, economical version of the Hegelian Idea. Mysticism does not come easily to the English temperament, and Green was no mystic. The concept of consciousness is derived from a fresh look at theories of knowledge, and Green tried to make it clear that

31. Murray Edelman, *The Symbolic Uses of Politics* (Urbana: University of Illinois Press, 1964), p. 19.

the immutable relations of true knowledge are the essential content of the ideal. Green occasionally seemed to endow the idea with properties of independence from human action, but never to the extent that Hegel did. Green was not taken in by the nationalist purposes to which Hegel's argument could be put. He commented: "Nor, unless we allow ourselves to play fast and loose with the terms 'spirit' and 'will,' can we suppose a national spirit and will to exist except as the spirit and will of individuals, affected in a certain way by intercourse with each other and by the history of the nation." [32] To the liberal way of thinking, it is to Green's credit that he translated as much of idealism as possible into a defense of voluntarism and positive liberty.

The part of Green's idealism which is hard to accept in the twentieth century is the belief in moral progress. It is probably the defeat of that charming nineteenth-century myth of progress which has destroyed the foundations of liberalism rather than the rediscovery of the darker side of human nature. A concept of progress is essential to Green's vision of an unfolding eternal consciousness. A more scientific study of human nature would indicate those elements of personality which are capable of beneficial development as well as of frustration. A characteristic of the human mental process is its capacity for symbolization and for adaptive behavior. These aspects of personality might be turned to the progressive purposes of idealism in somewhat the sense Green has in mind. The assumption of automatic progress is essential to Green's idealism, but not to the defense of liberal values. The potential for progress rather than the historical reality of progress is the crucial point in the justification of liberal values.

In the end, Green's moral idealism fails as a convincing justification for liberalism largely because his methodology does not probe the reality of human nature, relying instead on concepts as reality. Even as a moral philosopher, Green is guilty of logical errors too grievous to be ignored. The "true relations of knowledge" are too nebulous and undemonstrated to serve as a sufficient

32. Green, *Prolegomena,* pp. 193–94.

hook to hang a philosophy on. It may be that there is something about the social nature of humankind which can be elaborated into a justification for liberalism, but Green misses the mark when he joins those who base their premises about human nature on abstractions rather than on realistic analysis of behavior. Such a procedure makes for poorly founded justification of social norms.

At the same time, however, it must be said that Green provided liberalism with a number of powerful symbols around which activists could rally in the continuing quest to understand what liberty is, how equality can be furthered, and perhaps most important, where the state can become the agent for human development rather than simply the mediator of the conflict. For a more substantial resolution of these problems, we must turn to a whole new field of inquiry: psychoanalytic theory.

chapter three

Left from Right
in Sigmund Freud

Freud and Freudianism have penetrated our laws, humor, politics, and personal lives in an often unstructured and unsystematic way.[1] So we have to deal almost ex post facto with the phenomenon remarked upon by Herbert Marcuse: "psychological categories . . . have become political categories." [2] The works of Freud invite us to a kind of transaction in which we bring our need for political understanding to the test of his probing insights and perilous visions.

T. H. Green left us with ideals, but nothing convincing in the

1. A version of this chapter was presented to the Midwest Political Science Convention on April 29, 1972. Where citations are made here from *The Standard Edition of the Complete Psychological Works of Sigmund Freud,* rev. and ed. by James Strachey et al. (London: Hogarth Press and the Institute of Psychoanalysis, 1959 et seq.), only the volume number and pages are indicated. Where the title and date of the work are significant, they have also been included. Titles listed without the author are by Sigmund Freud.

2. Herbert Marcuse, *Eros and Civilization* (New York: Vintage, 1962). The effort to reconcile political science and psychoanalysis may once have suffered from the awkwardness Philip Rieff suggests: "Overawed by the energetic motions of the new science, a rather old and tired political science offers herself in a comically traditional marriage. . . ." Philip Rieff, "Psychology and Politics: The Freudian Connection," *World Politics,* Vol. VII, No. 2 (1955), p. 304.

way of analysis of human nature. Sigmund Freud told us much more than we might wish to know about our natures and, in the process, destroyed many of our ideals. Yet it is impossible to read Freud without sensing the richness and variety of human behavior. Human beings emerge in Freud's writings as subtle creatures capable of immensely difficult adjustments to life. To read Freud without the mediation of his critics is to see human nature animated, endowed with power and feeling far beyond the simple calculator image of the utile counters and contract rationalizers. Freud tells us not only about our rational behavior, but also the irrational; not only the conscious, but the unconscious; not alone our actions, but also our dreams.

Sheldon Wolin once commented that liberalism factored out the soul.[3] By that he justly demeaned the limited vision of Locke, Bentham, and the major figures of English liberalism. T. H. Green attempted to factor back in a kind of secular soul residing in the realm of the true relations of knowledge. Green was part of a larger movement, Hegelian idealism, which tried valiantly to raise humankind to the level of God by attributing spiritual properties to the mind.

If Freud tells us anything, it is that people are by no means godlike. Yet, at the same time, Freud makes us see that we are much more than simple processors of sense data. People act, choose, sublimate, plot, dream, and fantasize in ways incomprehensible to the English liberals and with motives horrifying to the German idealists. To the English tradition, Freud is a liberator of human instinct from the bondage of rationalism and empiricism. By the German tradition, Freud is a debunker of the transcendant and spiritual.

For the English, human nature is something less than the vivid and confusing self we all experience. For the Germans, human nature is more than human, rising to the throne of ultimates. Freud is more human than the English, less spiritual than the Germans,

3. Sheldon Wolin, *Politics and Vision* (Boston: Little, Brown, 1960), p. 341.

and more scientific than either. However, as we shall see, Freud's view was incomplete, and his contribution was mainly to bring the study of human behavior to the intimate laboratory of the clinic and so to turn the study of ourselves from analysis of concepts and symbols to analysis of behavior in the reality of life's struggles. Freud opened the door to a whole new vista of research and speculation.

In order to see Freud's contribution clearly, it is not enough to rehearse his basic concepts in the vacuum of expository prose. We need the focus of a specific problem. In discussing Green, we tried to look carefully at the relationship of individual and community. We will retain that focus but bring it closer by looking at the context of individual-community relations in contemporary liberal culture.

What, at root, characterizes the mental set of our culture? To a large extent, we are captives of the liberalism of Locke and Bentham. With them, we see life revolving around strategies for overcoming the scarcity of things we want, maintaining our individualism in the face of mass culture, and trying to restrain the seeming insatiability of our own appetites and those of others. We have, in short, a view of life that centers on struggle with alienated others in an alien environment. To mitigate the harshness of the struggle, we are socialized to possessive behavior—seeking independence from others in the presumed security of ownership. Society is presented as a great market for the exchange of goods and services. The adhesive of society is seen to be contracts enforced by the state for the limitation of "destructive" behavior.

C. B. Macpherson, Herbert Marcuse, and Sheldon Wolin, in delineating the reality of the liberal state, have done much to strip away the value symbols by which it is justified.[4] Liberty is really

---

4. Principally in C. B. Macpherson, *The Political Theory of Possessive Individualism* (New York: Oxford University Press, 1962), and *The Real World of Democracy* (New York: Oxford University Press, 1966); Marcuse, *Eros and Civilization;* and Wolin, *Politics and Vision,* esp. Ch. 9, pp. 286–351.

the freedom to compete without the assurance of an equal starting point. Equality is essentially impartiality in the enforcement of contracts, which themselves may be instruments of exploitation. I will begin, then, with the summary proposition that our culture is characterized by *scarcity economics* and *possessive individualism*.

To give these phrases systematic meaning, it is worth listing the ingredients more carefully in the form of assumptions and implications which stand behind the predominant form of the liberal tradition.

Assumptions

1. THE SCARCITY ASSUMPTION: There is an excess of demand over supply regarding the things people want out of life. The crucial significance of this is that existence must necessarily involve a struggle with the environment to wrest limited satisfaction from a world characterized by scarcity.

2. THE INDIVIDUALISM ASSUMPTION: Demands placed on life are inherently individual, arising from a basic drive for survival, as in Hobbes, or an abundance of personal appetites, as in Bentham.[5]

3. THE INSATIABILITY ASSUMPTION: Demands for gratification of desires are essentially unlimited—or if not unlimited, limited only by a level of satiation which is unacceptable in the face of general scarcity.[6]

Implications

1. THE POSSESSIVENESS IMPLICATION: Possession or ownership is the key to freedom. In "the relation of ownership," as Macpherson notes, "is freedom from dependence on the wills of others." [7]

---

5. Regarding Hobbes, see Macpherson, *The Political Theory of Possessive Individualism,* pp. 77–78. Regarding Bentham, see Wolin, *Politics and Vision,* p. 342.

6. Wolin, *Politics and Vision,* pp. 324–25.

7. Macpherson, *The Political Theory of Possessive Individualism,* p. 3.

2. THE MARKET IMPLICATION: The purpose of society is to establish and protect the market by which scarce goods can be allocated among conflicting demands. To the extent that there is to be equality, it consists, according to Sheldon Wolin, of equitable enforcement of the rules of an open market by those political authorities charged with its maintenance.[8]

3. THE CONTRACT IMPLICATION: Given the nature of possessive individualism, the polity is an artifice which requires the authorization of contracts backed by coercion to keep it in operation on an equitable basis. Without contract, "the enjoyment of the property [man] has in this state [of nature] is very unsafe, very insecure" (Locke).[9]

The classical liberals may be arrayed along a kind of continuum depending on their assessment of the seriousness of the competitive situation into which scarcity plunges us. The *Leviathan* (1651) is the grand solution to the problem of constant conflict Hobbes saw arising as a result of scarcity. Locke, somewhat more hopeful, appears as the advocate of contracts made by individuals with each other and collectively by the society with its trustees, the governors. Out of rational contracts, Locke argues, society can proceed in an orderly market to maximize the available utilities.

Ultimately we have Bentham, the democratizer of liberalism, who argues that individuals can assess their own utilities and that the function of political authority is to translate these assessments into policies. Bentham represents the high point of liberal individualism in the context of the market society, and what comes after in John Stuart Mill is a retreat to elitism, subjective value judgments, and, ultimately, to increased order imposed by the

8. Wolin, *Politics and Vision*, p. 347. On Hobbes, see also Macpherson, *The Political Theory of Possessive Individualism*, pp. 86, 93 ff, and John Locke, *An Essay Concerning the True, Original, Extent, and End of Civil Government, Second Treatise*, in *Great Books of the Western World*, Robert Hutchins, ed. (Chicago: Encyclopedia Britannica, 1952), Vol. 35, p. 25.

9. See John Locke, *Second Treatise*, in *Great Books*, Vol. 35, p. 53.

state as a remedy to the ravages of individualism. Mill retains the Draconian view of life as a struggle against nature.[10]

The significant point for this analysis is that Hobbes, Locke, and Bentham all shared in the assumptions behind the market society: the assumptions of possessive individualism.

If we may shift levels of inquiry for a moment, what has liberalism authorized? Whatever the rhetoric, individuals have come to be defined essentially and predominantly by their relationship to an inequitable market. The results of market competition are everywhere visible in class differences, racism, insecurity, exploitation, and repression.

The basic weakness of the free market is that the market itself is finally incapable of supplying equitable outcomes. Following Macpherson's analysis, there are two reasons for this. First, the market cannot yield outcomes in direct proportion to the expenditure by individuals of skill and energy, for the market has to reward ownership as well as skill and energy. Second, "the market can be shown to maximize utilities when a certain income distribution is taken as given. . . ." [11] It might be added that individuals can never have free access to the means of livelihood, for access is determined by the will of those who own the means of livelihood, and they can structure the conditions of access to suit their personal priorities once they have gotten an enterprise beyond the break-even point. Thus the paradox: the free market becomes a coercive master of our lives and fortunes.

All there is which can give comfort to humane values is the possibility of redistribution of results through some system of allocation. However, this requires a political process sufficiently insulated from the market that it does not simply convert market advantages into political advantages. Yet within the limits of the assumptions about human nature made by Hobbes and Locke, there is no possibility of such a thing occurring. How can possessive individuals who act in the market suddenly be transformed into advocates of

10. Regarding Mill, see his statement on an individual's relation to a hostile nature in Wolin, *Politics and Vision,* p. 317.

11. Macpherson, *The Real World of Democracy,* pp. 53–55.

equality and freedom in ways that would contradict and nullify whatever market advantages they may have acquired?

Liberalism, insofar as it is based on these assumptions, is a closed system. Minor variations aside, the development from assumptions of possessive individualism to the society of the utility-maximizers, the contract, and ultimately the Leviathan is a logical set-piece. The only prescriptions liberalism is left with are nostrums for the improvement of the efficiency of the market.

The basis for a new liberalism must be found in a different understanding of human nature. Freud opened up alternative possibilities by expanding our insight into the relationship between human behavior and scarcity. In these pages we will explore the ways in which Freudian ideas alter both the meaning and content of scarcity as well as the boundaries of possessive individualism.

The assumptions and implications listed above rest in the first place on observations of human behavior, however unsystematic. Freud will be treated here as a scientist who investigated human behavior. I will not treat Freudianism as a seamless web of theory partly because there are many seams indeed and partly because there is little reason to accept or reject Freudianism in toto. Some of his findings are closer to his clinical research than others. Some of his ideas arise from unabashed speculation and are therefore to be credited as the work of a great mind but subject to further testing and research.

It is obvious that I am trenching on the difficult question of the use of evidence about "the way things are" for normative conclusions about "the way things ought to be," a debate so well developed that it would benefit little from comment here. Suffice it to say that liberalism was formulated on a base of theory about human nature. It is legitimate then to comment on this theory in view of relevant research.[12]

Using the three assumptions of scarcity, individualism, and insatiability, and the three implications of possessiveness, the market

12. See Macpherson, *The Political Theory of Possessive Individualism*, p. 14.

view of society, and the necessity for contract, let us consider Freud's insights.

The Scarcity Assumption

Sigmund Freud accepts the phenomenon of scarcity as basic to human life.[13] The people Freud analyzed in his clinic were people who were starved for expressive outlets. To cite two examples of the significance of this for Freudian analysis, consider the phenomena of hysteria and dreams.

In 1888, Freud conceptualized hysteria as a symptom attributable to a paucity of outlets for the psychic energy. In an environment which cannot supply adequate possibilities for expressions, an individual suffering from acute excitation develops psychological aberrations.[14] In fact, the basic terminology of psychoanalysis represents categories of reactions to scarcity: repression, sublimation, anxiety. All of these refer to mental endeavors associated with the painful reality of insufficient gratification.

In 1894, Freud conceptualized the problem of hysteria as arising from an inability or unwillingness to convert desires into expressions (affect into discharge).[15] Freud's case studies are often tales of unfulfilled love and repressed sexuality ending in painful psychological and physical afflictions.

By 1900, Freud was ready to detail the results of scarcity for the process of dreaming: dreams are the expression of frustrated wishes distorted by censorship; scarcity of expressive outlets is a major factor in both the frustration of wish fulfillment and the censorship process.[16] There are also internal factors involved which will be dealt with later.

In 1905, Freud noted: "The source of an instinct is a process of excitation occurring in an organ and the immediate aim of the in-

13. *A General Introduction to Psychoanalysis* (New York: Garden City Publishing Co., 1943), p. 273; cited in Marcuse, *Eros and Civilization*, p. 16.
14. Vol. I, pp. 39–59 (1888).
15. Vol. III, pp. 43–68 (1894).
16. "The Interpretation of Dreams," Vol. IV, pp. 118–19, and Vol. V, pp. 550–72 (1900).

stinct lies in the removal of this organic stimulus."[17] The battle between instinctual expression and repression becomes the key to the differentiation of the mind into id, ego, and superego.[18]

So scarcity is very real and quite fundamental. But what is the nature of this scarcity, and is it necessarily immutable? One may distinguish between two types of scarcity in Freud.[19]

Primary scarcity arises from the association of the id with genital development. The desire for pleasure is stronger than the ability or willingness to deal with the implications of sexual activity.[20] The Oedipus complex is a study in scarcity. The child's explicitly sexual instinct emerges in relation to the mother, but direct sexual expression is perceived to be inhibited by the father and, later, by the taboos of society, until the child becomes in some way potentially capable of managing the consequences of sexual expression. It is the prohibition of gratification which triggers the Oedipus complex.

There is a secondary level of scarcity which stems from the lack of alternative outlets for sexual energy. Sexual energy which is blocked from expression through the primary processes of pleasurable release is sublimated and emerges as activity directed toward other objectives, such as acquisition of material goods or artistic endeavor. A society lacking sufficient secondary gratifications must necessarily be characterized by competition. Here lie the roots of social competitiveness in all fields of activity.

As Herbert Marcuse points out, elements of both the primary and secondary levels of scarcity are historically relative.[21] Opportunities for direct expression of sexuality vary according to cultural arrangements and levels of consciousness. Child-rearing customs have a considerable effect on the intensity and duration of

17. "Three Essays on the Theory of Sexuality," Vol. VII, p. 168 (1905).
18. "An Autobiographical Study," Vol. XX, pp. 30 ff. (1925).
19. See the distinction made in Herbert Marcuse, *Eros and Civilization,* pp. 117–26. Marcuse's distinction is more elaborate, as is his general discussion, because of his effort to bring Freud's entire metapsychology to bear on the discussion.
20. Vol. XX, p. 38.
21. Marcuse, *Eros and Civilization,* pp. 80, 120–22.

the Oedipus complex. In fact, Freud believed the results of the Oedipus complex may, through the phenomenon of the child's identification with the father, "turn into an expression of tenderness as easily as into a wish for someone's removal." [22] The sexual mores of a culture permit differing ranges of opportunity for sexual expression. The methods of controlling the reproductive consequences of sexual expression have undergone dramatic historical developments in recent times. Implicit in Freudian theory is the possibility of some kind of balance between psycho-physical development and opportunities for primary sexual expression.

Similarly, at the secondary level, the structuring of society to allow maximum possible expression of diverted sexual energy would reduce the impact of scarcity and provide a greater sense of liberation for each individual. [23]

The ominous implications of Freudian theory appear in the speculative works where Freud hypothesizes that the conversion of primary sexual energy into secondary expression is the motive force of civilization. It is this conversion which leads people to organize, to build, and to create those things essential to culture. There is the crucial assumption that a society which permitted maximum primary sexual expression would simply dissolve into lassitude and disorder for lack of these vital secondary activities. [24]

There is also the assumption that the institutions of civilization created at the second level must, in order to maintain themselves, repress primary sexuality as a means of conserving the energy which keeps civilization operating. This is, of course, the famous thesis of *The Future of an Illusion* and *Civilization and Its Discontents:* "To put it briefly, there are two widespread human characteristics which are responsible for the fact that the regulation of civilization can only be maintained by a certain degree of coercion—namely, that men are not spontaneously fond of work

22. "Group Psychology and the Analysis of the Ego," Vol. XVIII, p. 105 (1921).

23. See, for example, Freud's discussion on dealing with perversions in Vol. VII, p. 162 (1905).

24. *The Future of an Illusion,* trans. by W. D. Robson-Scott, rev. and ed. by James Strachey (New York: Anchor, 1964), p. 5 (1927).

and that arguments are of no avail against their passions." [25] It appears from this that civilization requires suppression, the keystone argument of the right.

Note, however, that there is an implicit optimum in Freudian theory between primary sexual gratification and secondary instinctual expression. The rightist implications of Freud's thought hold if, and only if, there is an inverse relation between primary sexual fulfillment and the decline of what may be called civilizing energy. To sustain this proposition involves a burden of proof never met by Freud. Furthermore, the statement cited above implies that a society which provided fulfilling work and opportunities for the constructive outlet of passions would require correspondingly less coercion.

Whatever its uses in "regulating civilization," suppression, the tool of the right, creates deprivations which, according to Freud's clinical theory, are as likely to lead to ill health as to the favorable mediation of the pleasure principle by the reality principle. The solution to both primary and secondary scarcity is a matter of creating opportunities for expression which do not endanger the reproductive function of the primary process or the civilizing function of the secondary process. The question of how to provide these opportunities in a world of scarce resources is, to repeat, historically relative. In fact, if Freud is right and sexual expression is primary in human life, the world's resources are not so scarce after all. Freud comments that "an individual man can himself come to function as wealth in relation to another one, insofar as the other person makes use of his capacity for work, or chooses him as a sexual object. . . ." [26] Conjecturing for a moment, the purpose of the economy is to support the process of instinctual expression by organizing support and security for sexual objects. This is the beginning of a formula for an intelligent allocation of resources, other than simply development for the sake of development. There is,

25. *Ibid.,* p. 6.
26. *Ibid.,* pp. 2–3. This comment occurs in the context of a formulation suggesting that "every individual is virtually an enemy of civilization"—a thesis dealt with later in the book.

further, the idea that a properly constructed community might well alleviate the scarcity of interpersonal expression.

Freud never offered any hope that such a rational solution would come about. But these grim forecasts are to be attributed to his later, speculative efforts. In the clinic, Freud helped his patients find ways of overcoming the crippling effects of scarcities. Beyond the therapeutic tools of psychoanalysis, there is the unmistakable implication that scarcity can be reduced once the dynamic of sexual energy is better understood.

The Individualism Assumption

Individualism is at the center of seventeenth-century liberal thought. Yet the liberal argument for the uniqueness of the individual is finally based not on any noble affirmation of the particular genius of each human being, but rather on the empiricism of Hobbes and particularly Locke.[27] Locke argued that we are the creatures of our senses. Differentiation in environment produces differentiation of individuals. Discounting Locke's natural law claims, individualism has no positive value; it is simply an artifact of differential sense perception. We are what we are almost by accident.

Psychoanalytic theory is likewise based on the idea that every individual is unique. Yet in Freudian theory, the individual does more than simply react to material stimuli; he or she deals with them in the context of internally generated impulses.[28] Human beings live in a world of psychic as well as sense gratifications.

An individual's mind is not simply a blank tablet upon which the

27. Wolin argues that liberalism, by affiliating itself so closely with market behavior, the "social denominator," actually wound up replacing individual conscience with social conscience at the expense of liberty. *Politics and Vision*, pp. 343–51.

28. Daniel Yankelovich and William Barrett point out that Freud's use of the term "mental" implies that there is something beyond the nervous system. They argue that it is not inconsistent with Freud's findings to hypothesize that one seeks out stimuli as well as merely reacting to them. *Ego and Instinct: The Psychoanalytic View of Human Nature*, rev. ed. (New York: Random House, 1970), pp. 42–43.

senses write, but rather an active mediator of psychic energy.[29] The basic psychological mechanisms of censorship and projection first delineated by Freud in his theory of dreams are purely mental operations. Freud even speculates in *Moses and Monotheism* that there is a kind of collective inheritance of "thought dispositions" and that succeeding generations embellish and develop these dispositions.[30] Whether or not there are inherited ideas of consequence for behavior, Freud reveals that our very perceptions become pleasurable or painful in relation to psychic reactions to instinctual pressures.[31] Thought consists of symbol formation.

Symbol formation is not simple coding of sense impressions; it is rather a means of attributing meaning to sense data in the context of internally generated drives and impulses. There is a certain majesty about the power of individual drives which emerges in Freudian theory, a majesty missing in the materialist reduction of individual designs according to Locke.

If liberalism factored out the soul, Freud factored it back in again by his research into the phenomenon of mental energy.[32] After Freud, it is no longer possible to view all individuals as simply consumer units in a market society—rather it becomes necessary to accommodate individual desires and designs in a new way. The fact that psychoanalytic theory reveals some of the patterns of these desires and designs allows some hope that this challenge can be met.

How does one move left or right on the matter of individualism? To argue for the rightist position is to argue that individual fulfillment comes from a proper relation to a hierarchical community. Each individual has a proper place in the scheme of society. On

29. Abraham Kaplan, "Freud and Modern Philosophy," in Benjamin Nelson, ed., *Freud and the Twentieth Century* (New York: Meridian, 1957), p. 211. See also Freud, *Moses and Monotheism,* trans. by Katherine Jones (New York: Vintage, 1939), p. 129; Philip Rieff, *Freud: The Mind of the Moralist* (Garden City, N.Y.: Anchor, 1961), p. 36.

30. *Moses and Monotheism,* pp. 126–27 (1939).

31. "Beyond the Pleasure Principle," Vol. XVIII, p. 11 (1920).

32. For a basic formulation of the concept of "mental energy," see "Studies on Hysteria," Vol. II, pp. 240–52 (1895). On the broader point, see Rieff, *Freud,* p. 6.

the left, by contrast, individuals are seen as ends in themselves contributing to a nonprescriptive community and deriving fulfillment from it as unique and valued members.

For Freud, instinctual drives may be combined differently in each individual, but satisfactions are both individual and relational. The fundamental proposition is that people live through relationships with other people. This is not quite the same as saying that individuals need the artificial structures of the state to be complete; and it is different also from saying that individuals are complete unto themselves.

To be sure, Freud's writing on the relation of human beings to groups reinforces a rightist argument for social control and elitism. These ideas are systematically developed out of an extension of some clinically based hypotheses in *Group Psychology and the Analysis of the Ego* (1921).[33] This venture into social psychology is predicated on the application of basic axioms of individual psychoanalysis to mass behavior. Through mechanisms such as identification and the collectivizing of the Oedipus complex, Freud arrives at some hypotheses concerning the leader principle. His essential argument is that groups are based on libidinal ties arising from the frustration of instinctual drives.[34] The unsatisfactory resolution of the Oedipus complex leads individuals to band together and to act out collectively what they cannot resolve privately: the limitation of the power of the father-leader, or, in extreme cases, his removal.[35]

It is against this background, that Freud makes a dramatic proposal: "Let us venture, then to correct [the idea] that man is a herd animal and assert that he is rather a horde animal, an individual creature in a horde led by a chief." [36] What we have here is

33. *Works,* Vol. XVIII, pp. 67–193 (1921).
34. *Ibid.,* pp. 113–24.
35. *Ibid.,* pp. 120–21. See also Freud's treatment of the origin of ethics in *Civilization and Its Discontents,* ed. and trans. by James Strachey (New York: Norton, 1961), p. 90 (1930). See also Rieff, *Freud,* pp. 301–2, and Norman O. Brown's imaginative inflation of these ideas in *Love's Body* (New York: Vintage, 1970), pp. 3–32.
36. XVIII, p. 121 (1921).

nothing more or less than a *venture* founded upon an *assertion*. Whatever the explanatory value of the horde as a metaphor for mass behavior, whether it is of partial or total utility, Freud has only the scantiest of systematic evidence to support his hypothesis. It is a *possible* extension of his clinical theory to social psychology and nothing more.

In any case, to say that the human being is a horde animal in the context of Freud's argument is not precisely the same as saying that the individual cannot be seen to have intrinsic merit apart from a relationship to a hierarchical community. Horde behavior is viewed as a secondary response to instinctual drives. To the extent that clinical research is relied upon, horde behavior may be seen as one of a number of possible responses to the deprivation of gratification. *The Authoritarian Personality,* among other works, reports on that phenomenon in fascist Germany.[37] There is also the possibility of the individual dealing with deprivation internally through repression, sublimation, and alternative expression. The reasons Freud was led to such a dramatic conceptualization of group behavior are traced by Rieff to his reliance upon such outright polemics as Gustave Le Bon's *The Crowd,* an elitist argument from design founded on no reliable research.[38]

Yet, paradoxically, it is in the relational nature of individual existence that one finds the beginning of a leftist argument on the point of individual behavior with respect to scarcity. Horde behavior is a neurotic response to instinctual frustration. Alternatively, there are such phenomena as fulfilling and liberating human relationships achieved through persistence and creative human effort. Reviewing his findings in 1921, Freud allowed that "in the development of mankind as a whole, just as in individuals, love alone acts as the civilizing factor in the sense that it brings a change

37. Theodore W. Adorno et al., *The Authoritarian Personality* (New York: Harper, 1950), p. 675; see also Marcuse, *Eros and Civilization,* pp. 185–86.
38. Philip Rieff, "The Origins of Freud's Political Psychology," *Journal of the History of Ideas,* Vol. XVII, No. 2 (1956), pp. 235–49. Cf. Paul Roazen, *Freud: Political and Social Thought* (New York: Knopf, 1968), pp. 218–32.

from egoism to altruism. And this is true both of sexual love for women, with all the obligations which it involves of not harming the things that are dear to women, and also of desexualized, sublimated, homosexual love for other men, which springs from work in common." [39] The reality is that inter-individual relationships contain the potential for both love and hate, but hate is a response arising from a compensation for deprivation. Scarcity as a factor in individual relations enters partially, and possibly largely, as a result of malformed social conditioning. The hierarchical prescriptive community which Vienna was in the late nineteenth century could hardly be identified as a situation in which opportunities for positive and meaningful relationships were maximized.

Freud's clinical research takes us beyond the simple model of individual isolation most clearly seen in Hobbes with his dire vision of natural life as a war of all against all. There is nothing in Hobbes's assumptions about human nature to suggest that two people acting together might be mutually liberating (other than as allies against a common enemy). The random isolation of individuals presumed by empiricism does not provide any real explanation of inter-individual relationships. Indeed, the solution to the most basic kind of scarcity is found not in the individual subordination of interests to the social contract, but rather in the development of mutual relationships based on self-expression at the very deepest level. Freud himself theorized that these interpersonal relationships are the strongest defense against horde behavior.[40]

Yet, again, Freud explicitly rejects the proposition that sexual instinct can serve as a sufficient basis for community. In *Totem and Taboo* (1913), Freud comments that

> Sexual needs are not capable of uniting men in the same way as are the demands of self-preservation. Sexual satisfaction is essentially the private affair of each individual. The asocial nature of neuroses has its genetic origin in their most fundamental purpose, which is to take flight from an unsatisfying reality into a more pleasurable world of

39. "Group Psychology," Vol. XVIII, p. 103.
40. *Ibid.*, p. 140.

fantasy. The real world, which is avoided in this way by neurotics, is under the sway of human society and of the institutions collectively created by it. To turn away from reality is at the same time to withdraw from the community of man.[41]

It is worth repeating that Freud is condemning "unsatisfying reality" associated with repressive institutions. Presumably institutions supportive of mutually gratifying relationships would not create the aversive patterns of antisocial behavior which lead to neurosis.

There is, in addition, a contradiction in this passage. The whole thesis of psychoanalytic thought rests on the proposition that the gratification of the sexual instinct is basic to self-preservation. "The demands of self-preservation" cannot finally be separated from instinctual gratification. It is in the ordering of primary and secondary gratification that community arises—and these two levels are inextricably linked. The flight from reality Freud speaks of is a metaphor which has no factual basis by the terms of his theory. There is no such thing as pure expression of the id; the ego (with its reality orientation) and superego once created never disappear. All that can be said is that there are more or less strategic discharges of instinctual energy. Calculation is a part of every expression. It remains to be argued whether the preponderance of these calculations leads people toward or away from an equitable community, a topic for the section on the market implication.

The Insatiability Assumption

It is the insatiability assumption which brings us directly to the question of coercion. If individual demands are insatiable, or satiable only at a level unacceptable in the face of general scarcity, then there is an obvious need for some social mechanism for the restriction of demand levels. The less self-control, the greater the need for social control if scarcity is to be dealt with rationally. The right argues that self-control is minimal and large amounts of so-

41. "Totem and Taboo," Vol. XIII, pp. 73–74 (1913).

cial control are necessary. The left takes the reverse position, although here, as elsewhere in this argument, the difference between right and left is a matter of degree rather than of logical opposites. In addition to the relatively obvious issue of control of instinctual expression, there is another issue of crucial significance for the debate. Is instinctual gratification necessarily exploitative of others? Or does gratification finally require nonexploitative shared relations between individuals? Once again the answer lies along a continuum of possible combinations.

Freud is best known as a theorist of the instincts. It was in a departure from the roughly similar concept of innate ideas that Lockean empiricism originated. Sigmund Freud forces a reconsideration of that departure. The whole edifice of psychoanalytic theory rests on the proposition that life is a constant drive for instinctual gratification. But the detail on that edifice is a complex explanation of how the pleasure principle is modified, channeled, and redirected.

On the face of it, and at a distance, it seems Freud is arguing for the rightist position that the demand for pleasure is insatiable. Human beings are guided first and foremost by the pleasure principle.[42] The reason is that life begins with the rude shock of separation from the secure and pleasurable world of the womb. The effort to restore that utopian world of total gratification in the face of a hostile world becomes the essential enterprise of life.[43]

Given the profoundly individualistic origin of the pleasure instinct, it would appear that exploitation of others in the process of gratification is inevitable. It probably is, but again it is a question of degree. The answer to the question depends very heavily on the rest of what Freud discovered about instinctual gratification. Furthermore, exploitation is more than an inter-individual phenomenon. An environment which represses gratification also exploits.

Let us examine these themes more carefully. We will try to establish several important propositions: (1) Instincts are internally

42. Vol. XVIII, p. 7.
43. Norman O. Brown, *Life against Death* (New York: Vintage, 1959), p. 31.

generated, shaped by a powerful system of internal controls, and conservative in direction; (2) instincts are flexible in expression, subject to relatively better or worse environmental responses, and more likely to be satiated at a lower level in the absence of obstacles to fulfillment; (3) finally, instincts are reliant upon mutually gratifying nonexploitative relationships for their fullest expression.

The Oedipus complex is a manifest adaptation of the pleasure instinct to the necessity for control. This leads to a more inclusive set of controls:

> In the course of individual development a part of the inhibiting forces in the outer world becomes internalized; a standard is created in the Ego which opposes the other faculties by observation, criticism, and prohibition; we call this new standard the *Super-ego*. From now on, the Ego, before undertaking to satisfy the instincts, has to consider not only the dangers of the outer world, but also the objections of the Super-ego, and has therefore more occasion for refraining from satisfying the instinct.[44]

Whether the internalization of the prohibitions of the father is really the model for all ensuing inhibition of instinctual fulfillment remains an open question.[45] The explanatory power of the Oedipus formulation is such, however, that it can be assumed to account for at least the first phase of self-control.

Where the environment is maladapted to these vital beginnings, the individual can become locked in a repetition compulsion. This amounts to an effort to restore, in sublimated form, the pleasurable realm of childhood by recreating the form of a specific childhood situation, though the context in which this is done may cause nothing but pain. In his clinical work Freud uncovered powerful evidence that some adult human pathologies reflect archetypes derived from the Oedipal conflict. Lasswell's case studies of politicians provide additional evidence.[46] What remains uncertain is

44. *Moses and Monotheism*, pp. 149–50 (1939).
45. The position is reviewed in *ibid.*, p. 153; see also the more extensive discussion of instinctual control in *Civilization and its Discontents*, pp. 21–32.
46. Harold Lasswell, *Psychopathology and Politics* (New York: Viking, 1960, originally 1930).

whether this is a general and inevitable phenomenon or whether it is characteristic only of neurotics of the type Freud observed in his clinic and Lasswell in his case studies.

Psychoanalysis as therapy assumes that the illumination of repressed incidents will enable the ego to deal with them rationally rather than neurotically. The objective of psychoanalysis is normality, not in the sense of a statistical average, but in the creation of an appropriate balance of control and expression. Freud makes clear the balancing function of the ego in *The Ego and the Id* (1923):

> It [the ego] is entrusted with important functions. By virtue of its relation to the perceptual system it gives mental processes an order in time and submits them to "reality-testing." By interposing the processes of thinking, it secures a postponement of motor discharges and controls the access to motility. This last power is, to be sure, a question more of form than of fact; in the matter of action the ego's position is like that of a constitutional monarch, without whose sanction no law can be passed but who hesitates long before imposing his veto on any measure put forward by Parliament. All the experiences of life that originate from without enrich the ego; the id, however, is its second external world, which it strives to bring into subjection to itself. It withdraws libido from the id and transforms the object-cathexes of the id into ego-structures.[47]

Whatever the changes in Freud's view of the id-ego-superego triad, the basic theme of control remains. Summarizing the clinical literature, Anna Freud lists nine methods of ego defense against the id: "regression, repression, reaction-formation, isolation, undoing, projection, introjection, turning against the self and reversal, . . . [and] sublimation, or displacement of instinctual aims." [48]

While Anna Freud has cataloged these developments of psychoanalytic theory and added to them, the roots are in Freud's earliest work. There is, for example, his account of "screen memories"

47. *Works,* Vol. XIX, p. 55; cf. p. 25 (1923).
48. Anna Freud, *The Ego and the Mechanisms of Defense,* rev. ed. trans. by Cecil Baines (New York: International Universities Press, 1966), pp. 42–53.

which deals with the selective uses of memory to overcome instinctual challenges and, later, his account of the purposive characteristics of everyday forgetfulness.[49] The point is, instinctual discharge occurs amid a complex of influences and controls.

There is another implication of Freud's view of instinct and pleasure which is most significant: *instinct is conservative*. In fact, instinct is conservative by definition:

> *It seems, then, that an instinct is an urge inherent in organic life to restore an earlier state of things* which the living entity has been obliged to abandon under the pressure of external disturbing forces; that is, it is a kind of organic elasticity, or, to put it another way, the expression of the inertia inherent in organic life.

> This view of instincts strikes us as strange because we have become used to seeing in them a factor impelling towards change and development, whereas we are now asked to recognize in them the precise contrary—an expression of the *conservative* nature of living substance.[50] [Freud's italics.]

Were the instincts unmediated by other psychological functions, it is obvious that one's instinctual nature would commit an individual to an impossible existence. The condition to which instincts would have the self return is clearly unattainable. However, there is mediation, partially described above, and there is gratification short of a relapse to inertia. What is needed is the strengthening of this internal mediation together with the creation of optimum levels of gratification.

It now becomes necessary to consider Freud's differentiation of the life instinct and the death instinct.

In *Beyond the Pleasure Principle* (1920), an admittedly speculative work, Freud introduces the death instinct by a rather bizarre reference to the relation between organismic life and the sun which concludes with the declaration: "If we are to take it as truth that knows no exception that everything living dies for *internal* reasons

49. "Screen Memories," Vol. III, pp. 301–22 (1899), and "The Psychopathology of Everyday Life," Vol. VI, pp. 269–90 (1901).
50. "Beyond the Pleasure Principle," Vol. XVIII, p. 36; cf. pp. 40–41 (1920).

—becomes inorganic once again—then we shall be compelled to say that *'the aim of all life is death'* and, looking backwards, the *'inanimate things existed before living ones.'* " [51] The three ideas that we die of our own volition, that there is a continuously acting volition or impulse to seek death, and that a part of the death instinct is its explicit desire to regress to an inanimate state, are antithetic to the idea of human liberation as the left has generally thought of it.

On the other hand, Freud is involved here in a rather dubious form of theorizing. That cells have chemical processes which sustain organic activity for only a limited time is not a necessarily compelling basis for hypothesizing that *intention* is associated with the degeneration of these processes. It is possible, and even likely, that severe mental stress may mortally afflict the physical system, but are there really adequate grounds for arguing that people die because they will to die?

The real political significance of the death instinct lies in its relationship to aggression. In his famous letter to Einstein, Freud offers both a summary of his theory of aggression and a bleak forecast of the future of humanity.[52] In this formulation, the death instinct appears to have two sources. There is the argument cited above that the death instinct is a psychic analogue of the degenerative process of cells. There is also the attribution of the death instinct (and its externalized expression labeled the destructive instinct) to the repression which originates in the Oedipus complex.[53] So long as this destructive instinct is one of a series of

51. *Ibid.,* p. 38.
52. "Why War?," Vol. XXII, pp. 199–215 (1933); see also "Thoughts for the Times on War and Death," *Collected Papers,* trans. by Joan Riviere (London: Hogarth Press, 1949), Vol. IV, pp. 288–317 (1915).
53. Vol. XXII, p. 211. See also *The Ego and the Id,* Vol. XIX, pp. 40–41, 58. On the other hand, Anna Freud explores the possibility that the mechanism of projection by which we attribute our own aggressive acts to others might also be a mechanism by which we can form "valuable positive attachments. . . . This normal and less conspicuous form of projection might be described as 'altruistic surrender' of our own instinctual impulses in favor of other people." *The Ego and the Mechanisms of Defense,* p. 123. Sigmund Freud comments in his *Autobiography* that his concept of sexual

possible responses to repression, it can be argued, as Freud does in the Einstein correspondence, that it can be mitigated through alterations in social responses to instinctual expression. In his essay, "Thoughts for the Times on War and Death" (1915), Freud also argues that a change in attitude toward death could facilitate a reduction in the warlike outlet of aggression.[54]

To the extent, however, that there is an inevitably aggressive impulse which specifically demands destructive behavior for its expression, we have the grounds for ultimate pessimism. It is here that Freud must rely on his argument by analogy to physical processes, and it is here also that Freud is furthest from his clinical research. Freud's prognosis in the letter is pessimistic, but it is in the context of his plea for a change in social institutions: "An unpleasant picture comes to one's mind of mills that grind so slowly that people may starve before they get their flour." [55]

As it happens, Freud is more typically impressed by the flexibility of human instincts. The choice of objects varies widely and Freud was not willing to argue consistently that instincts are separable into precise categories.[56] Rather, the normal human being acquires in the course of development a widely diversified repertoire of objects upon which to discharge instinctual energy.[57]

impulses is broader than genital drives: "I hope it will have been easy to gather the nature of my extension (on which so much stress has been laid and which has excited so much opposition) of the concept of sexuality. That extension is of a twofold kind. In the first place sexuality is divorced from its too close connection with the genitals and is regarded as a more comprehensive bodily function, having pleasure as its goal and only secondarily coming to serve the ends of reproduction. In the second place, the sexual impulses are regarded as including all of those merely effectionate and friendly impulses to which usage applies the exceedingly ambiguous word 'love.' I do not, however, consider that these extensions are innovations but rather restorations: they signify the removal of inexpedient limitations of the concept into which we had allowed ourselves to be led." Vol. XX, p. 38.

54. "Thoughts for the Times," *Collected Papers,* Vol. IV, pp. 316–17.

55. "Why War?," Vol. XXII, p. 213. See also *Civilization and Its Discontents,* p. 88.

56. See Rieff, *Freud,* p. 31n.

57. For a summary of Freud's position on instinct as of 1915, see Yankelovich and Barrett, pp. 36–37.

Most of his clinical insights portray this flexibility. Freud's early work on dreams can be seen as an example of how the individual adopts a substitute satisfaction, dreaming, so one can accommodate a physical need for rest. We dream, so we can sleep.[58]

Given the flexibility of instinctual discharge, it is again apparent how important the accommodation of culture to human nature is. Freud makes an interesting observation in *Three Essays on Sexuality:* "The most striking distinction between the erotic life of antiquity and our own no doubt lies in the fact that the ancients laid the stress upon the instinct itself, whereas we emphasize its object. The ancients glorified the instinct and were prepared on its account to honour even an inferior object; while we despise the instinctual activity in itself, and find excuses for it only in the merits of the object." [59] Cultural norms and mores have a great deal to do with the levels at which satiation may be found, and the obvious lesson here is that repressive prudery is unlikely to be healthy.[60] Taboos, for example, are in some ways a rational, though surely an excessive response.[61]

It becomes clear that obstacles to instinctual fulfillment are particularly likely to be dysfunctional if they are not associated with alternative outlets. Freud comments, "It is easy to show that the value the mind sets on erotic needs instantly sinks as soon as satisfaction becomes readily obtainable. Some obstacle is necessary to swell the tide of the libido to its height." [62]

The proposition of the right that instinctual behavior can in fact be suppressed is defied by this argument. All that can be done is to provide the most constructive and acceptable possible outlets for instinctual expression. The fruits of simple suppression are sickness and exploitative behavior. In this context, Herbert Marcuse argues for a new "rationality of gratification." The logic is

58. "On Dreams," Vol. V, pp. 666–80 (1901).
59. "Three Essays on the Theory of Sexuality," Vol. VII, p. 149 (1905).
60. See "Types of Onset of Neurosis," Vol. XII, pp. 227–28 (1912).
61. "Totem and Taboo," Vol. XIII, pp. 34–35.
62. "The Most Prevalent Form of Degradation in Erotic Life," in *Collected Papers,* Vol. IV, p. 213, cited in Herbert Marcuse, *Eros and Civilization,* p. 207.

that all social arrangements must be put to the test of their utility in promoting a rational gratification of instincts, and this test, he states, "creates its own division of labor, its own priorities, its own hierarchy.[63]

Culture is advanced by this kind of rationality.[64] It is when personal or cultural rationality becomes an end in itself apart from the spontaneity of life that it becomes exploitative. The vision of Sigmund Freud is that, in the words of H. Stuart Hughes, "it would eventually prove possible to train the instincts to nonrepressive living." [65] When Freud attacked ethics, he was not attacking rationality as a guide to human behavior but rather the pathology of externalized faith versus the constructive possibility of rational internal understanding.[66]

Finally, the limit on instinctual satiation is, to return to an earlier theme, the inter-individual nature of fulfillment. Sexual energy is precisely the desire to combine in sensuous union with another. The establishment of a fully gratifying relationship involves a commitment both to the similar demands of another individual and the formation of a community capable of serving such a relationship. Meeting these requirements is a task which brings the social behavior of individuals into nonexploitative modalities. The strategic calculus of instinctual gratification through satisfying mutual relationships is the element in Freud which opens the way to a less repressive society which could potentially realize the central values of the left.

It must be noted that Freud, especially late in his life, was pessimistic about human rationality. In *Moses and Monotheism* (1939), he comments, "The human intellect has not shown itself elsewhere to be endowed with a very good scent for truth, nor has the human mind displayed any special readiness to accept truth. On the con-

63. Marcuse, *Eros and Civilization,* p. 205. See also Rieff, *Freud,* p. 204.
64. See Erik Erikson, *Childhood and Society,* 2d ed., rev. (New York: Norton, 1963), pp. 185–86.
65. H. Stuart Hughes, *Consciousness and Society* (New York: Knopf, 1958), p. 137.
66. Rieff, *Freud,* pp. 139, 319–20. See also Brown, *Life against Death,* pp. 147–48.

trary, it is the general experience that the human intellect errs very easily without our suspecting it at all, and that nothing is more readily believed that what—regardless of the truth—meets our wishes and illusions halfway." [67] Yet this does not prevent him from developing the psychoanalytic technique which is really a device, not for improving a repressive rationality, but rather a means for understanding the logic of gratification. In works such as *Civilized Sexual Morality and Modern Nervous Illness,* Freud has paragraphs of prescriptions for ways in which repressive social arrangements can be humanized.[68] The very logic of his position is that instincts will seek the most satisfying possible outlets and that humanity will rebel against those social arrangements which constrain self-expression.

Freud's basic discoveries came in the context of a Victorian society. Women in particular were exploited by the double standard of an elitist male chauvinist civilization. The rebellion Freud witnessed took the form of widespread female hysteria.[69] Human beings confronted with more gratifying alternatives for instinctual expression will accept them, providing the confrontation is managed so as to reach their own level of calculation as Freud was occasionally able to do in his clinic.

Implications

So far, I have examined some themes in Freud's clinical research which bear on the liberal view of the human condition. The argument has been directed to the possibility that the leftist interpretation of Freudian thought is better supported by the evidence which emerged from his research than the rightist view. Freud's clinical findings and the theory associated with them have been credited more than his later generalized psychological explanations

67. *Moses and Monotheism*, p. 166.
68. "Civilized Sexual Morality and Modern Nervous Illness," Vol. IX, pp. 181–204 (1908). See also Ernest Jones, *The Life and Work of Sigmund Freud* (New York: Basic Books, 1957), Vol. 3, pp. 336–37.
69. Erik Erikson, *Insight and Responsibility* (New York: Norton, 1964), pp. 31–33.

of social phenomena. While Freud's theories changed over time, I have tried to rest the major points of analysis on his most elementary insights.

If the argument so far be accepted, then it is possible to continue the inquiry by considering some possible modifications of the central implications of possessiveness, the market-based society, and contract. To review for a moment, the scarcity assumption has been modified by the point that scarcity is historically relative, essentially interpersonal rather than commodity oriented, and, finally, relievable partly through self-understanding of the appetites and their expression.

The individualism assumption is enriched in Freudian thought through a restoration of the psychic uniqueness of individuals in relation to their environment. Humans are seen as actors rather than as simple processors of sense data. Furthermore, individuals acquire primary meaning and gratification in their lives not in isolation but rather in relationships with other individuals.

As for the insatiability assumption, we have seen that Freudian clinical theory is a study in the control of instinct. We find, additionally, that instincts are conservative, flexible, partially relative to environment, satiable at a lower level in the absence of obstacles, and limited by the requirements of interpersonal relationships.

What does this mean for possessiveness, the market, and contract?

The Possessiveness Implication

In classical liberal thought, freedom is essentially seen as freedom from the wills of others, and it is thought to be achieved through the possession of those things which satisfy appetites. Thus, economic self-interest becomes the essential calculus of liberal political thought.

In the first place, Freud could see that there is no such thing as independence from the wills of others. The nature of life is relational. We live in a complex of relationships, some of the most important of which originate in childhood. Life is not so much a search for security as it is a search for expression. Security is exceedingly significant, but clinics are full of people who have demolished their hopes of security when starved for expression. Similarly, the content of economic self-interest changes considerably depending upon what individuals see themselves needing. People make widely varying choices about how hard to work and how much to accumulate, and an even wider array of decisions about how to spend what they accumulate. The logic behind self-interest, Freud would have us understand, is the logic of instinctual expression, rather than the logic of conventionally defined acquisitive behavior.

Freedom in psychoanalytic theory is not freedom from the wills of others so much as freedom from the repression of the self. In fact, Norman Brown suggests that the very pursuit of economic independence through possessiveness may be isolating and psychologically damaging. Individual possessiveness divorced from its relationship to personal needs is the opposite of liberating, it is enslavement of instinctual energy to inert objects.[70] Ultimately, the very ideal of complete freedom from the wills of others is antihuman.

The Market Implication

Recall Wolin's thesis that the market society is the final expression of liberalism. The purpose of such a society is to establish, protect, and legitimize the market by enforcing equitable rules of access so that scarce goods can be allocated among conflicting demands. Implicit in this perspective is the notion that the market is a neutral social mechanism. The normal must compete with the neurotic, the aggressive, and the exploitative. To the extent that the market is regulated only by the rule of equal access, the trade-offs in the market place will be unlimited. If all things are permitted, individual dignity, health, and even survival, will be traded for basic needs.

What Freudian theory suggests is the beginning of a formula for

70. Brown, *Life against Death*, pp. 293–94. See also a similar argument in Wolin, *Politics and Vision*, pp. 333–34.

the regulation of the market. It is predictable that an exchange system which begins as a free market will soon become a system in which those who acquire advantages will use them to structure the market so as to ensure their preeminence. Freudian theory directs us instead toward a consideration of the kinds of behavior which are acceptable in the marketplace. What kind of regulation will permit the market to operate as an exchange system for real human needs under conditions which are not degrading and repressive? There are few specific answers in Freud, but he has located, it seems to me, the real questions.

Furthermore, the regulation of the market place requires not simply the prevention or elimination of certain kinds of behavior. Rather, society must take steps to provide for basic human needs. The operation of the market must be regulated, and the outcome of the market must likewise be structured, at least partially, so that severe deprivation is avoided. This is not the command of charity; it is a rational requirement for the protection of the basic exchange mechanisms of societies.

The Contract Implication

The essence of contract is the provision of substitutive compensations in the event the primary obligations of an agreement are unfulfilled. Liberal theorists assumed that binding contracts enforced by the state were necessary to contain the vagaries of individual behavior. Once again, a simplistic view of human nature led them to endorse an unregulated power of contract. Constrained by materialist assumptions, these theorists saw contract as a means of stabilizing society.

What Freud provides is the beginning of a standard for determining which contracts are valid expressions of human nature. The validity of contract consists only in those agreements which are fair to the needs of the parties, realistic in the demands placed upon them, and appropriate in the means of alternative compensation allowed. No individual can expect protection from the state for contractual obligations damaging to that individual or to others.

Freud has made us see that individuals do not always act in their own self-interest. They may well act out of anxiety, hostility, or neurosis. A legitimate process of contract depends as much upon state enforcement of procedures and compensations as it does on the regulation of the substance of contracts. With no regulation of substance, the contractual process will be debased and lose its legitimacy. It will become a repressive instrument of civilization.

Conclusion

Throughout this discussion, conjecture has been mingled with analysis. At this point, the amount of conjecture will be increased as the impact of the rethinking of scarcity is explored.

Considering the leftward direction of the argument, I have been rather freely using the term regulation, which is earlier associated with the right. The distinction which needs to be made is between suppressive regulation and compensatory regulation. The argument of the right is that antisocial instinctual behavior must simply be suppressed. Freud points out that this is inhumane as a philosophical position, and unsuccessful as a practical matter.[71]

Compensatory regulation, on the other hand, involves the provision of alternative outlets for activity which is proscribed. The state which operates by the principle of compensatory regulation attempts to deflect dysfunctional behavior through education and, in more serious cases, counseling. Repression is employed only in clear cases of behavior which is fundamentally exploitive of the processes of social interaction, and then only through separating the individual from the occasion of dysfunctional behavior to a situation in which remedial steps can be taken. Thus, compensatory regulation has a claim to legitimacy which simple suppression of some behavior in favor of preferred behavior does not.

In addition, compensatory regulation limits the state to those forms of authority which are necessary to the maintenance of basic social processes of interaction. As for behavior by individuals

71. "Civilized Sexual Morality . . .," p. 192.

which affects only themselves, the state cannot enforce an arrangement, for example, a contract, which has that effect, nor can it act to prevent it by simple suppression. The role of the state is to provide those processes by which the individual can learn the consequences of certain varieties of instinctual expression. Beyond that, the function of the state is to provide maximum outlets for nonexploitative expressive behavior. Individual freedom is dependent upon release from repression of the self, and this is, in part, a matter of structuring the environment as well as a matter of allowing the individual maximum freedom of choice in the form and style of self-expression.[72]

The foregoing takes little account of Freud's more speculative metapsychological theories. Herbert Marcuse, on the other hand, argues that metapsychology is crucial to the formation of a revolutionary philosophy. In weighing these opposing contentions, it is important to understand that Freudian metapsychology is largely derived from a model developed in physics. Freud speaks frequently of the "mental apparatus" as a kind of energy converter. As Erik Erikson suggests, the basic models in his writings emerged in relation to the "dynamic-economic" principle.[73] The mechanistic implications of the model were turned to occasionally successful uses in the clinic. It is when Freud collectivizes his concepts and speaks of groups and civilizations responding as individuals do and acting out the functions of the mental apparatus that the burden of proof vastly overwhelms the evidence Freud has at his disposal.

The reason for Freud's devotion to a mechanistic model of the mental apparatus is probably to be found in the simple fact that he was a doctor who tried to cure the body by manipulating the mind. His patients came to him with physical ailments which appeared not to be susceptible to normal physical treatment. Freud's enterprise in life was to find those links between the physical and the mental apparatus which would serve as lines of diagnosis and therapy. As long as he researched the direct connections between

72. Cf. Roazen, *Freud,* p. 256.
73. Erikson, *Insight and Responsibility,* pp. 41–42.

mental experiences and physical symptoms in individuals, he found keys to the universality of human nature. Erik Erikson, who followed through on the genetic scheme begun in Freud, tells us a great deal more.[74]

As a scientist of collective behavior, however, Freud transposed conversion processes operative in individuals to the mass. When the mass becomes the unit of analysis rather than the individual, then Freudian theory becomes metapsychology on the grand scale. Freud did no research on mass behavior; rather, he fitted his science of individual behavior to his unsystematic observations of the social and political turbulence of his time. The best that can be said of the scientific merits of these studies is that they are richly hypothetical.

The principal obstacle to the development of a political theory from Freud's writings is that he never got past considering the state as a psychological object in the context of his Oedipus formulation. He was clearly trying to deflate the extravagant claims made for the sanctity of the state by the German idealists and at the same time attempting to explain, as best he could, how his ideas related to war. Freud objected to socialism on the ground that it was not sufficiently realistic about the psychological dimensions of power. He was willing, on the other hand, to endorse the idea of a change in people's attitudes toward property.[75]

As we have tried to show, there is a great deal in Freud which suggests the possibilities for both the content and form of political regulation. Indirectly, though still significantly, Freud implies the

74. Erikson, *Childhood and Society,* pp. 48–108, 247–74; for a later formulation, see Erikson's *Identity: Youth and Crisis* (New York: Norton, 1968), pp. 91–141.

75. Speaking of the need for a decrease in aggressive behavior, Freud is reported to have commented, "I think it unquestionable that an actual change in men's attitude to property would be of more help in this direction than any ethical commands; but among the Socialists this proposal is obscured by new idealistic expectations disregarding human nature, which detract from its value in actual practice." Cited in Jones, *Life and Work of Sigmund Freud,* Vol. 3, p. 343. The comment noted by Jones seems to conflict to some extent with remarks in *Civilization and Its Discontents,* pp. 60–61, and in "Why War?," Vol. XXII, pp. 211–12.

need for considerable change in the way organizations utilize human talents. Total devotion to efficiency and economic rationality are not likely to result in intelligent, responsive decision-making and work performance. One must approach organizations with the same wariness that the ego displays in dealing with the superego.

Marcuse is right, it seems to me, in arguing that Freud held little hope for salvation through individualism. Marcuse argues that concentrating simply on individual potential is not adequate to the need for a rethinking of political philosophy. The environment does play a massive role in individual development, but the essence of the environmental role is in inter-individual relationships formed out of the needs of participants in society.

There is a tendency on the left to argue that obstacles can be removed through a revolutionary transformation of the environmental setting. However, revolutions (or even "transformations") are simply large-scale coercive enterprises involving massive exploitation of some by others. The psychological consequences of revolutionary change are repression and its attendant behavioral aberrations. Marcuse correctly belabors some Freudian revisionists for overlooking the conditioning influence of social institutions as a major factor in creating the problem.[76] But it is also true that the process of changing social institutions is fraught with opportunities for exploitation and repression. The state cannot enforce individual relationships in a mode favorable to Freudian normality. Rather, in the last analysis, it can only create the circumstances for their development. The behavioral sciences can guide the formation of state policy in this respect, though they cannot dictate what is unacceptable to a public without engendering the very behavior reforms should be designed to prevent.[77]

76. Marcuse, *Eros and Civilization*, pp. 219–20.
77. In defense of the dialectical nature of Freudian thought and even its "poetry," Brown suggests that psychoanalysis can never be a science because "Empirical verification, the positivist test of science, can apply only to that which is fully in consciousness; but psychoanalysis is a mode of contacting the unconscious under conditions of general repression, when the unconscious remains in some sense repressed." *Life against Death*, p. 320. However, Freud was intensely empirical in his clinic. He built his theory

The intervening variable between the status quo and orientation to change must be the very unhappiness which Freud thought was the normal lot of humanity. The catalyst for change must be research in human behavior which is well grounded and presented intelligibly with a due regard to prevailing sensibilities. The focus needs to be on what social arrangements will alleviate repression without increasing the burden of manipulation.

Insofar as the possibilities for nonexploitive expression are increased, the state may indeed wither away, that is, in those areas where it has too closely regulated individual behavior. The role of the state may well increase, on the other hand, in the area of directing a collective attack on the scarcity of the means of survival. The attack on this basic problem is already heavily collectivized through corporate power. The question remains whether equity can result from the private control of the means of overcoming scarcity. It may be that private power in the market can be sufficiently regulated if the standards of public accountability are very high. Failing that, the socialization of the means of production is called for, though it will take intensive effort to prevent the advance of repressive bureaucracy in those circumstances. Critics on the left frequently point to the capacity of our technology to overcome the scarcity of basic commodities. It hardly needs to be pointed out that this technology does not operate independently of a psychological and cultural setting. Freud's contribution is to indicate some of the prerequisites for a rational productive process which serves the purposes of both producers and consumers.

Freud does not provide a rationale for minimizing the importance of scarcity. He does, however, expand both the meaning of scarcity and our understanding of the costs of a variety of strategies

on systematic observation and tested it in therapy. Brown's definition of science is too restrictive. The clinic is also a scientific laboratory; and it was Freud, above all, who described, classified, and even measured, through a detailed symptomology, the properties of the unconscious and their relations to psychic and physical phenomena. Conscious behavior and inadvertent behavior provide systematic clues to the content of the unconscious. What remains, of course, is far more elaborate research and verification.

for living with it. After Freud, it is at the very least much more difficult to argue that the free market society of classical liberalism is adequate to the resolution of the problems of survival, let alone the problem of establishing a legitimate political order.

What remains are the big questions: How do people relate to one another? Is there any basis for building a state on a theory of human mutuality? How is it that human consciousness develops, and what is its content? These questions must take us further into the development of psychoanalytic and psychological knowledge.

chapter four

Of Human Mutuality
and Social Control

Sigmund Freud opened the way to a new language of justification with his fundamental investigation of human behavior. The changing view of sex in Western culture is only the surface manifestation of a much deeper revolution in the way the educated individual looks at humanity. Repression, sublimation, neurosis, and many other psychoanalytic terms have nearly become household words. Individuals in our society commonly justify their actions by referring to these concepts. The courts and the penal system increasingly recognize the psychological dimensions of crime. Organized religion is in a perpetual state of intellectual crisis partly because of the Freudian critique of the uses of ethics. God has been socialized, de-mythologized, and even dethroned in modern theology.

Freud's insights are powerful. He makes us see that scarcity in human life is not exclusively material and that we live in a web of highly potent personal relations. He is the pioneer theorist of childhood and of the residues childhood leaves in the unconscious. Yet the crux of the problem remains: how does the individual relate to a community? To know the answer to that question requires a more comprehensive understanding than Freud makes available, particularly if we are searching for a positive theory of human mutuality. We need to know more about the nature of the social tie than the mechanics of the Oedipus complex. At the same time, we must find a clearer account of the way society controls our behavior. It is the ignorance of mutuality and of social control which hobbles traditional liberal theory. In their emphasis upon the individual, Locke, Bentham, and Mill leave us with only a partial account of human nature. Green, with his abstracted vision of social purpose, demonstrates the weakness of traditional liberalism without revealing the innards of human behavior.

Freud leaves us with essentially three interrelated problems: (1) an unsatisfactory theory of human mutuality, (2) a negative account of social control functions, and, most critical (3) an incomplete theory of the life cycle and its roots in human nature. In this chapter the first two problems will be considered in relation to the works of George Herbert Mead and B. F. Skinner. The third problem, the vital question of the life cycle, will largely be reserved for the next chapter on Erik Erikson.

There are many other psychological theorists who might well be considerd here: Jung, Adler, Sullivan, Piaget, Horney, Roheim, Reich, and Marcuse, to name a few. Mead is included because he is a pioneer in the development of social psychology. Mead discusses the formation of personality through role-taking, a principal point of access for a political theory based on human mutuality. Skinner is considered in this study partly because his thought seems hostile to liberal individualism and partly because of his insights into the nature of social control. Skinner's theory of social conditioning has almost been converted into a political theory in its own right. Erikson, a neo-Freudian, reinterprets psychoanalytic theory through an elaboration of the stages of human development. These three transformed psychoanalytic and psychological theory.

Liberation theory must overcome the central muddle of liberalism. Liberals really have no theory of community, only a theory of association. The basis of this association is material interest in property. Sometimes, at least, the thought is parent to the act, and liberal society has come to be characterized by an almost compulsive attention to the advancement and protection of property interests. It has long been popular on college campuses to decry materialism, and many among the most recent generation of students have gone into the world disposed to do something about it by establishing communes, returning to the land, and foregoing the consumption mania of middle-class life. These experiments are brave and even rewarding. However, simple denial of material interest will not solve the problem. Material interests have to be placed in the context of a larger understanding of the nature of the communal tie.

Institutions have to be redesigned either from within through a refusal to act out the prescribed patterns, or from above through intelligent leadership—or both. Every institution in American society has undergone some kind of transformation in the last decade. The church has its Berrigans, the universities their radical activists, the business world its Ralph Naders, and politics its Gene McCarthys and George McGoverns. Labor unions puzzle over the qualitative demands of young workers. Organizations of all kinds feel the pressure of new life styles and challenges to orthodoxy.

These transformations have been only partly successful in most cases, and everywhere there is confusion about which way to proceed. As is the rule with social experimentation, not all the results have been good. Part of the reason may be found in the mood of this putative social revolution: it is a mood of rejection. Somehow there is a feeling that people have been moved out of the center of society to be replaced by routines. The rejection of routine is a painful act, the more painful if there is no positive theory of what to replace it with. Rather than simple rejection, or perhaps as a sequel to it, the time has come to find solidly grounded theories of social mutuality. George Herbert Mead pioneered in such an understanding, and his fundamental concepts are still basic to social psychology.

An Evolutionary Psychology of the Self

George Herbert Mead (1863–1931) attempted to synthesize the two major intellectual revolutions of the immediate past: Freudianism and Darwinism. Mead used evolutionary concepts to explain the psychodynamics of self-construction. The socialization of basic impulses through contact with others is the primary focus of Mead's theory. He supports this analysis with observations on the symbolic properties of language.

An understanding of his synthesis requires a brief examination of the basic concepts of impulse, the significant symbol, the generalized other, and the relation of all three to linguistic analysis. Mead's philosophic positions on epistemology and pragmatism contribute further elements to a solution.

Mead explains the rise of the self in an evolutionary context. "Human behavior . . . springs from impulses," he claims. "An impulse is a congenital tendency to react in a specific manner to a certain sort of stimulus, under certain organic conditions. Hunger and anger are illustrations of such impulses." Mead prefers the term *impulse* to Freud's conceptualization of *instinct* because impulses are modified extensively in the course of life. Mead sets the stage for a discussion of impulse modification through stimulus and response.[1]

Individuals do not simply act out the repertory of their impulses. Something intervenes in the expression of many impulses. The central intervening factors, according to Mead, stem from a process of mental reflection beginning in childhood with the taking of roles. Children identify with others in their range of contacts. The responses of others give meaning to symbolic gestures. The demands of others and the constraints of shared meanings shape the expression of impulses. Thus the child begins to understand the primordial condition of development: social limits on behavior.[2]

From this rudimentary social experience, the child comes to be a reflective creature and achieves the beginning of a *self*-conscious-

1. George Herbert Mead, *Mind, Self, and Society* (Chicago: University of Chicago Press, 1934), p. 337. The use of Mead to supplant Freud's theory of mutuality is not original to this argument. See Anselm Strauss's introduction to *George Herbert Mead on Social Psychology* (Chicago: University of Chicago Press, 1964), p. xii.

2. Mead, *Mind, Self, and Society*, pp. 141n, 365–66; Mead, "The Mechanism of Social Consciousness," *Journal of Philosophy*, Vol. IX (1912), p. 404.

ness. "For [the child] enters his own experience as a self or individual, not directly or immediately, not by becoming a subject to himself, but only in so far as he first becomes an object to himself just as other individuals are objects to him or in his experience; and he becomes an object to himself only by taking the attitudes of other individuals toward himself within a social environment or context of experience and behavior in which both he and they are involved." [3]

It is obvious enough that we are social creatures, but several centuries of liberal thought ignore the mechanics of such a fundamental part of the human condition. Perhaps that is why our social life is so often constrained by not knowing just how to break that barrier of isolation which we so carefully construct.

Mead provides an analytical crossing of that barrier. His major analytic concepts are the "significant symbol" and the "generalized other." The idea of the significant symbol is that the self emerges from the process of developing shared meanings with others. Mother, father, and siblings provide the child's referents for symbolization. Later, teachers, friends, and relatives become important. Through the process of acquiring and creating shared symbols, the child learns to see his or her own impulses from other points of view. The individual works out conflicts in these interpretations to arrive at action. The contradictory quality of much human action is explained by unresolved conflicts among the images of the self assimilated from several sources.[4]

The "generalized other" is a slightly more complex and intriguing notion. Mead says, "The organized community or social group which gives to the individual his unity of self can be called 'the generalized other.' " [5] The generalized other is a role apart from any individual role-player—though individuals such as policemen,

---

3. Mead, *Mind, Self, and Society*, p. 138; cf. p. 354.
4. *Ibid.*, p. 149. Verba's work with small-group theory emphasizes the importance of "opinion leaders" who become a kind of "significant other" for the purpose of opinion formation. Sidney Verba, *Small Groups and Political Behavior: A Study of Leadership* (Princeton, N.J.: Princeton University Press, 1961).
5. *G. H. Mead on Social Psychology*, p. 218.

teachers, and judges may be perceived primarily as representatives of the generalized other. Mead's concept approximates what others refer to as the norms of the community. Mead argues that impulses are frequently interfered with and shaped by the acquired habit of referring to the generalized other.[6] We have the testimony of the archetypal middle-class life style as evidence. "What will the neighbors think?" "They say he's a bad person." "I don't want to look like a fool." "I like it, but it's different."

There are more systematic empirical correlates to these theoretical constructs found in analyses of opinion formation. Festinger's concept of a *strain to consistency,* which summarizes the likelihood that individuals will harmonize personal opinions with group views to avoid "cognitive dissonance," fits with Mead's analysis of the generalized other.[7] Jewell and Patterson review a series of group-role orientations in legislative behavior. Such roles as "ritualist, tribune, inventor, broker, and opportunist" suggest that several generalized and significant others may be relevant in determining individual actions in complex political situations.[8] Converse finds that two principal constraints on opinions are, first, the degree of positive feeling toward the belief system as a whole, and second, membership in an interest group. It is reasonable to suggest that the belief system represents the *generalized* other and the interest group a *significant* other.[9] Lane and Sears, synthesizing research on opinion formation, identify the conflict between a particularly valued source (commanding especially significant shared meanings) and group membership as a major arena for the working out of opinions.[10]

The stretchability of Mead's concepts in the face of considerable

6. Mead, *Mind, Self, and Society,* pp. xxviii.

7. See discussion in Verba, *Small Groups,* pp. 23–24, and the bibliography in Robert Lane and David Sears, *Public Opinion* (Englewood Cliffs, N.J.: Prentice-Hall, 1964), p. 45n.

8. Malcolm Jewell and Samuel Patterson, *The Legislative Process in the United States* (New York: Random House, 1966).

9. See Philip Converse, "The Nature of Belief Systems in Mass Publics," in David Apter, ed., *Ideology and Discontent* (New York: Free Press, 1964), Ch. 6, pp. 206–61.

10. Lane and Sears, *Public Opinion,* pp. 53–54.

behavioral research indicates their limited utility as operational concepts, but it also demonstrates the major significance of individual reaction to specific sources as well as to abstracted summations of group attitudes. The latter point is crucial to the philosopher. The self is considerably more than the sum of an individual's opinions—the self is also an action system, existing in a web of pressures.

Mead thought language was the key to unraveling the role-taking process. The emerging self uses language symbols as a way of participating in common meanings. ". . . (the) human self arises through its ability to take the attitude of the group to which he belongs—because he can talk to himself in terms of the community to which he belongs and lay upon himself the responsibilities that belong to the community; because he can recognize his own duties as against others—this is what constitutes the self as such." [11] The self learns to depend on symbols which bring about desired responses from relevant others. At the same time, the self authors its own pattern of responses to the stimulus of significant symbols.[12] In this sense, symbolic interchange makes the mind. Language creates us even as we learn to use it. In emphasizing the psychological and philosophical significance of language, Mead is part of the twentieth-century movement to relate human conduct and linguistic analysis.[13]

Individual role-taking occurs in two modes. One mode is *reactive*. The individual reacts to roles he or she perceives others taking. The content of the reaction originates with the impulse involved in the confrontation with the other. A second mode of behavior arising from role-playing is *empathetic*. The self takes the

11. *G. H. Mead on Social Psychology*, p. 33.
12. *Ibid.*, p. 185; see also Mead, *Mind, Self, and Society*, p. xxi.
13. For some specific comments on the significance of language which incorporate Mead's perspective, see Edward Sapir, *Selected Writings in Language, Culture, and Personality* (Berkeley and Los Angeles: University of California Press, 1960), pp. 12–13; "A Study in Language and Cognition," by Roger Brown and Erik Lenneberg in Sol Saporta, ed., *Psycholinguistics* (New York: Holt, 1961), specif. p. 493; and Joseph Church, *Language and the Discovery of Reality: A Developmental Psychology of Cognition* (New York: Random House, 1961), pp. 86–87.

role of the other. An individual, in a sense, moves out of the self and looks back upon it and its impulses from a different perspective. The easiest illustration is the child playing at being a parent. A child admonishing a sibling or a doll can sound very parental indeed. We seldom find ourselves in one mode to the exclusion of other. Language, with its vast array of symbols, permits rationalizations and expressions which reflect both modes while binding us to common meanings.[14] As we play roles, the symbols we use mold and socialize us. To speak is to realize human mutuality.

Mead's thought constitutes a descriptive structure within which much, if not all, human behavior can be fitted. By relating *impulse* through *language* to *role-taking,* Mead constructed a powerful argument for the sociality of human nature. Impulse refers to one's biological nature; role-taking and language provide both abstract and empirical referents for describing the individual's psychological dimensions. As Charles Morris points out in his introduction to *Mind, Self and Society:* ". . . Mead endeavored to carry out a major problem posed by evolutionary conceptions: the problem of how to bridge the gap between impulse and rationality, of showing how certain biological organisms acquire the capacity of self-consciousness, of thinking, of abstract reasoning, of purposive behavior, of moral devotion; the problem in short of how man, the rational animal, arose." [15]

For our purposes, it is enough to note that Mead demonstrates how human behavior is shaped in a broader social context than Freud's Oedipus complex indicates. What Freud describes is one of life's most powerful role-playing situations. Freud's claim that all subsequent socialization is carried on as a symbolic extension of the Oedipus complex may be considered doubtful. Mead establishes a conceptual framework for looking beyond the Oedipus complex to other formative relations between the self and others. At the same time, Mead supports the liberal argument that each individual is unique. No two individuals share an identical field of others and of significant symbols. Mead also moves beyond crude

14. Mead, *Mind, Self, and Society,* p. 376, cf. pp. 150–51.
15. *Ibid.,* pp. xvi, 347.

biological determinism by suggesting that biological impulses are heavily modified by the socializing experience.

There are two other important respects in which Mead helps form a new kind of liberationist theory. Mead supports the essential argument of an idealist theory of knowledge. He is also a scientific pragmatist.

To ask the question "How do people acquire knowledge?" is to get close to the core of human nature. Traditional liberalism is nowhere so frightening as in its reduction of mind to sense-data processor. The consumer is the prototype of liberal man. John Locke might have found today's highly organized shopping centers a basic expression of social interaction. Yet the self we experience seems somehow impoverished by this caricature. Sense impressions may be powerful, but are they the final determinants of behavior? Arguments about theories of knowledge can get pretty abstruse, but there is enough at stake for the understanding of self and society to justify a brief consideration.

Where do the complexities of mental invention come from? Green struggled to lift knowledge from the province of the senses, yet he shows us only that we can agree on certain kinds of abstractions without telling much about how we get to that point. It is Mead who brings psychology to bear on what the mind is made of. His trend of argument falls in the same broad class of theories of knowledge. He is an idealist—but a sophisticated one.

Mead's theory of knowledge involves an important deviation from the orthodox idealist position, but it is a deviation which considerably strengthens the validity of idealism. Mead points to several aspects of thinking which cannot be explained by the empiricist argument, particularly in its materialist form. His basic insight is that thinking "is a process of conversation with one's self when the individual takes the attitude of the other. . . ." [16] In the mind's interior, there is something more sophisticated than a calculator of purely material sense impressions.

The human mind is an active agent limited only by the selectivity of perception. The selectivity arises both from the physical limita-

16. Mead, *Social Psychology*, p. 38.

tions of the individual and from the socialization received in the role-playing process.[17] Within those limits, the analytic function of human knowledge emerges from the perception of stimuli which trigger conflicting impulses—a position which materialists might be able to cover by stretching their categories. But the "representation" function by which individuals compare their possible reactions against their role environment would seem to be out of reach of even the most convoluted materialist categories.[18] We not only think, we analyze options reflectively. Through thought, individuals can even escape the hands of the present. Ideas are tested against imagined future possibilities. In fact, ideas themselves are shaped by incorporating a time dimension.[19] The *self-reflexive* character of knowledge, in both its social and temporal dimensions, is the essence of Mead's argument against an empiricist theory of mind.[20]

Orthodox idealism relies on the concept of a form of universal mind, often with religious connotations. Green, it will be recalled, located the eternal factor in the universal truth of certain relations of knowledge. He transposed this into the "eternal consciousness." Mead rejects what might be called the *eternity principle* of idealism. His criticism is that idealist fail to specify how this could be so in fact, and they do not specify the mechanism by which the mind comes into its capacity for abstraction.[21]

Rather, Mead says the patterning of idea structures comes from the commonality of psychological development. We acquire our uniformities as human beings who develop through a matrix of shared relationships.

The demise of the eternity principle in idealism should not cause any lamentation among liberals. It is precisely that feature of German idealism which supported the mythological excesses of fascism. Wagner's operas symbolized for a generation the legends

17. *Ibid.,* p. 191.
18. Mead, *Mind, Self, and Society,* p. 357.
19. *G. H. Mead on Social Psychology,* p. 181.
20. For a critique of Mead's treatment of epistemology, see Maurice Natanson, *The Social Dynamics of George Herbert Mead* (Washington: Public Affairs Press, 1956), pp. 61, 80–81.
21. Mead, *Mind, Self, and Society,* pp. xiii–iv.

of a collective spirit beyond knowledge and mortality itself. Mead's social psychology permits a vision of the self as more than a sensual utility-maximizer and, at the same time, less than an agent of the eternity principle. We are humans who think, symbolize, and relate intimately with others.

Mead's rejection of orthodox idealism places him within another basic movement in the twentieth century: pragmatism. He believed in the development of cumulative knowledge through science. In that way, he shared in the nineteenth-century myth of progress.[22] In a review of Le Bon's *The Crowd,* he criticizes the "program-ism" of socialism in favor of the "opportunism" of pragmatic science.[23] We have seen enough since Mead's time of the misuses of science to be skeptical of the idea that the progress of science necessarily yields progress for humanity. But it is also undeniable that humankind has accumulated knowledge through science far faster than was possible under the weal of religion.

The specific importance of pragmatism for this argument is that it indicates where and how to look for an argument to justify a new vision of liberation. If there is any central message in pragmatism, it is that the question of purpose must be resolved by reference to experience rather than abstraction. The methodological premise of this book is that scientific knowledge must be used more effectively to support normative understanding. Mead's investigation of people's social creativity clearly implies that one's *purpose* or essential design is to be a social creature.

The Limits of Mead's Psychology

Useful as Mead's descriptive framework may be, it does not rest directly on empirical evidence, and it does not provide the heart of a philosophical system in the form of a specific account of purpose in human life.

22. Shibutani Tamotsu, "George Herbert Mead," *International Encyclopedia of the Social Sciences* (New York: Macmillan, 1968), p. 87.
23. George Herbert Mead, "The Psychology of Socialism," *American Journal of Sociology,* Vol. V (1899), pp. 406–9.

George Herbert Mead pioneered in establishing the conceptual groundwork for social psychology. At the time of his eminence there were few systematic experiments on human behavior to support the formulation of generalizations. He often alludes to the patterned activities of children and the symbolic properties of language to illustrate his theories, but there is little rigorous testing reported in his lectures.

This methodological weakness would be significant if it were not for the fact that later research demonstrates the powerful utility of role theory. Some contributions which illustrate the point are those of March, Simon, Crozier, and Thompson on organizational behavior; Masters and Huitt on legislative behavior; Eldersveld on political parties; and Edelman on political language and role-taking. Common themes characterize these works. The roles played by individuals are often derived from reactions to roles played by others. The taking of roles is frequently justified by referring to expectations generated by other individuals and by group interests. The pursuit of individual needs is heavily modified by estimates of role implications.[24] All of this reinforces Mead's view that institutions are "social habits." [25] Mead's thesis that the personality is *en-*

24. See James March and Herbert Simon, *Organizations* (New York: Wiley, 1958), p. 183, on goal adjustment arising from comparison with other individuals and organizations; Jewell and Patterson, *The Legislative Process,* p. 400, on the interplay between role perceptions and the group environment in legislative relations; Victor Thompson, *Modern Organization* (New York: Knopf, 1961), p. 116 ff. on the ideological, dramaturgical, and bureaucratic role responses to specialization; Michel Crozier, *The Bureaucratic Phenomenon* (Chicago: University of Chicago Press, 1964), p. 194, on the manipulation of communication difficulties for the reinforcement of roles; Nicholas Masters, "House Committee Assignments," *American Political Science Review,* Vol. LV (1961), pp. 345–57, on role expectations and their correlates to interests in congressional committee systems; Ralph Huitt, "The Congressional Committee: A Case Study," *APSR,* Vol. LXVIII (1954), pp. 342–43, on roles played for public and private consumption; Samuel Eldersveld, *Political Parties: A Behavioral Analysis* (Chicago: Rand McNally, 1964), Chapters 1, 10, 11, on the political party as a reciprocal deference structure; Murray Edelman, *The Symbolic Uses of Politics* (Urbana: University of Illinois Press, 1964), Ch. 7, on political language, and Ch. 8, on persistence and change in goals as a function of group role identity.

25. *G. H. Mead on Social Psychology,* p. 31.

tirely formed by social experiences may not be validated now or ever, but the overwhelming impact of role structures on individual behavior is not to be doubted.

The social psychology of George Herbert Mead establishes a useful descriptive framework for broadening understanding of human nature, but it does not solve an essential problem in the justification of humane values. The difficulty is in his discussion of the directionality of human behavior. There are two ultimately conflicting components to Mead's ethical theory: the idea that individual impulses are the basic reference point, and that some impulses are conducive to social relations while others are injurious. Mead attempts to resolve the problem:

> If we look at the individual from the point of view of his impulses, we can see that those desires which reinforce themselves, or continue on in their expression, and which awaken other impulses, will be good; whereas those which do not reinforce themselves lead to undesirable results, and those which weaken the other motives are in themselves evil. If we look now toward the end of the action rather than toward the impulse itself, we find that those ends are good which lead to the realization of the self as a social being. Our morality gathers about our social conduct.[26]

Mead is probably wrong on empirical grounds about the likelihood of antisocial impulses losing out in the reinforcement process. For example, rigidities caused by neurosis in individuals and forms of hysteria in groups may intervene in the self-adjustment of evolution. If that is so, Mead's view raises and does not solve the old problem of private advantage in conflict with the general good.

Mead argues that the morally right act is one in which individuals behave with the best interests of others as well as themselves—but what exactly are those interests? People collectively must act so as not to limit and restrict the opportunities for manifold role identification in society.[27] But what of individuals whose

26. Mead, *Mind, Self, and Society*, p. 385.

27. *Ibid.*, pp. 383–84, 379; George Herbert Mead, "Natural Rights and the Theory of the Political Institution," *Journal of Philosophy*, Vol. XII (1915), pp. 148–51. See also Mead, *Mind, Self, and Society*, pp. xxxii–iii,

role-environments may have placed their role-formulation at odds with the society's interests? Mead indicates how that happens by illuminating the uniqueness of an individual's collection of significant others. There is every likelihood that individuals will develop conflicting personalities only partly attenuated by the influence of generalized other(s).

To the extent that Mead's collective ethic argues for open social processes, he assists the justification of liberationist values. We admit to having a considerable stake in the development of good arguments for open social processes based on equality and liberty. Consequently, such an argument is properly included in liberation theory.[28] However, the issues of allocating state resources, establishing a structure of obligation with limits on permissible behavior, and constituting the arrangement of authority in the state cannot be solved satisfactorily unless there can be an imperative reconciliation of individual and social interests. As Erik Erikson suggests, "There is an optimum ego synthesis to which the individual aspires; and there is an optimum societal metabolism for which societies and cultures strive." [29] Mead describes a vital mechanism of individual and social interaction. He advances understanding of the relation between "ego synthesis" and "social metabolism" even if he doesn't specify an "optimum" which knits both together.

Mead is important because he goes beyond the restrictive framework of Freudianism in specifying the mechanism of human mutuality. Self and society are interdependent. The id may dominate the structuring of role relationships in childhood, but Mead's framework establishes role-taking as a general mechanism. Subsequent empirical research demonstrates that the mechanism is significant throughout life. Mead places the impact of community on

xxv–xxvi. For a critique, see Natanson, *Social Dynamics of George Herbert Mead*, pp. 67–68, 87.

28. See Henry Kariel, "The Political Relevance of Behavioral and Existentialist Psychology," *APSR*, Vol. LXI (1967), p. 341, for a discussion of the relevance of this point to behavioral and existentialist psychology. Thomas Landon Thorson offers a related argument from an epistemological point of view in *The Logic of Democracy* (New York: Holt, 1962).

29. Erik Erikson, *Young Man Luther: A Study in Psychoanalysis and History* (New York: Norton, 1958), p. 254.

the self in a more intelligible perspective than Freud's sublimation theory.

Mead's argument serves well as a number of basic values. Persons are seen as *rational* animals utilizing complex role mechanisms to calculate the implications of impulses. Each individual is *unique* in the accumulation of role perspectives. The profound interdependence created by mutual role-taking implies an argument for *equality*. At the same time, since individuals owe their personalities largely to the influence of others, we have social obligations on the basis of *mutuality*. *Liberty* is important because human self-development cannot occur without a free play of intelligence in a context of alternative role possibilities. Mead gives preliminary form to a number of arguments which will be refined in the discussion of Erik Erikson. Mead's thought may not comprise a complete political theory, but it does take us a long step toward laying the conceptual groundwork while at the same time indicating the major remaining tasks.

Evolution, Operant Conditioning, and Social Control

B. F. Skinner's thought is conveniently summarized in *Science and Human Behavior.*[30] *Walden Two,* written in the form of a novel, serves as a platform for staged debates on Skinnerian principles.[31] *Beyond Freedom and Dignity,* his most recent book, largely replays and only occasionally extends his previous arguments.[32] Skinner broadens the framework for understanding processes of evolutionary human adaptation.[33] The substance of his contribution is a system of operational definitions for the study of human behavior. These definitions are oriented toward reducing the room left for "explanatory fictions," his epithet for references to processes internal to the organism. Skinner fills in the evolutionary scheme for

30. B. F. Skinner, *Science and Human Behavior* (New York: Free Press, 1953).

31. B. F. Skinner, *Walden Two* (New York: Macmillan, 1948).

32. B. F. Skinner, *Beyond Freedom and Dignity* (New York: Vintage, 1971).

33. Skinner, *Science and Human Behavior,* pp. 90, 434–35.

explaining human behavior by showing us analogies to the "natural selection" principle.[34]

Skinner defines the self as "simply a device for representing a *functionally unified system of responses.*" [35] Skinner makes no assumptions about the content of those responses. For Mead, the central stimulus-response pattern revolves around role-taking, primarily through language. In Skinner's view, Mead's theories become one hypothesis among many testable in studying human behavior. It is clear from the outset that Skinner has little to offer on the question of human purpose which will assist in defining political norms. What Skinner does propose is a method for accumulating information about the reality of human behavior. It is hard to think of a reason for being opposed to finding out more about human behavior. There are more substantial implications in Skinner's thought however, and it is important to illuminate the structure of his ideas and their consequences for the discussion of social control. We will return to the question of human purpose and Skinner's effort to deal with it.

It is customary to discuss B. F. Skinner in the framework of the stimulus-organism-response (S-O-R) model. According to the usual generalization, Skinnerism means concentrating on stimulus and response as a way of minimizing or denying the independence of the organism. Skinner's contribution to the science of stimulus-response observation is the concept of *operant behavior.* The term "operant" is meant to emphasize the relationship between a particular response and the reinforcement of that response.

Skinner focuses on the consequences of behavior. To reinforce by reward a particular act is to increase the likelihood of similar future acts. The probability factor supplies Skinner's unit of measurement. Evolution is the history of the reinforcement patterns the species encounters—limited, of course, by the genetic origins of the species. If the reinforcement of specific operant behavior ceases, that class of responses will diminish even to extinction. It is possible to chart the "extinction curve" as a function of the

34. Skinner, *Beyond Freedom and Dignity,* pp. 15–16.
35. Skinner, *Science and Human Behavior,* p. 285.

diminution of reinforcement.[36] Skinner's conceptual repertory of operant behavior, response, reinforcement, and probability operationalizes an experimental science of human behavior.[37]

In the course of charting extinction curves and patterns of behavior, Skinner has found that positive reinforcement is a more powerful tool for the control of behavior than negative reinforcement. It is more effective to reward than to punish. Punishment generates emotional reactions in human beings which create a persistence in operant behavior which can overcome the pain of punishment. Likewise, withholding rewards leads to extinction much faster than introducing punishment. Skinner's argument is a potent rejoinder on empirical grounds to those conservatives who say that humans are evil and the evil must be punished if the good is to emerge.[38]

So far Skinner seems to be within the liberationist fold. But the hitch is that Skinner's categories really amount to a conceptual conspiracy against the possibility of human freedom.[39] As will be shown below, Skinner at times hedges on whether there is anything left to the human organism which cannot be explained by operant reinforcement. But the drift of his argument is that "The hypothesis that man is not free is essential to the application of scientific method to the study of human behavior." [40] Of course Skinner cannot prove that the pattern of reinforcement makes the person. That proposition is in the class of unprovable generalizations. The *degree* of conditioning remains an open question even if the final answer may not be accessible by the experimental method.[41] The essential point to be understood about Skinner is that he demonstrates the power of environmental factors on behavior in a very

36. *Ibid.*, p. 72.

37. *Ibid.*, pp. 64–65. For an illustration, see *Walden Two*, pp. 116–28.

38. Skinner, *Walden Two*, p. 260.

39. See, for example, Skinner's discussion of "creativity" in *Science and Human Behavior*, pp. 228–29, of "thinking" on p. 252, and of "private events" on p. 282.

40. *Ibid.*, p. 447, cf. *Walden Two*, p. 256.

41. Skinner, *Walden Two*, p. 257.

convincing empirical framework. The question which must concern liberals seeking to justify their values is how to deal with the phenomenon of environmental influence on human behavior.

Skinner claims, "We all control, and we are all controlled." [42] With or without government intervention, much if not all of our behavior is controlled by the reinforcements in our environment. Skinner effectively argues that the old question of whether to create an instrument of control in forming a government is misdirected. The only question is, "Who shall control?" Our behavior is being manipulated by the educational system, ad agencies, the family, corporations, interest groups, and churches, as well as by governments. Each social institution participates in the pattern of social control by organizing its own brand of reward and punishment. Skinner wants to rationalize the phenomenon of social control by linking it to an empirically justifiable ethic.[43] Here he joins Dewey, Mead, and others in the tradition of pragmatic ethics. We are invited to experiment to see what reinforcements lead to behavioral patterns conducive to happiness.

Skinner would invest behavioral scientists with power and let them control the experimenting, a step John Dewey proposed early in this century.[44] In *Walden Two,* the planners try to maximize a priori values like happiness, voluntarism, security, and creativity while testing internal priorities and the priorities of these values with respect to others. The argument is appealing, but it should also be realized that Skinner has to assume a value starting point in order to launch the system at all. His defense of the values he starts with is generalized and commonsensical.[45]

Democratic pluralists urge a diversification of social control to prevent any institution or individual from acquiring sufficient power to control us in a manner adverse to our interests. A "polyarchy" characterized by bargaining is supposed to protect free-

42. Skinner, *Science and Human Behavior,* p. 438, cf. p. 240.
43. *Ibid.,* p. 433.
44. See John Dewey, *The Public and Its Problems* (Denver: A. Swallow, 1954).
45. Skinner, *Walden Two,* pp. 251–76.

dom.[46] The other possibility is that pluralism results in a chaotic environment in which essential tasks are ignored and individuals are manipulated by many masters for reasons having nothing to do with their welfare. As Skinner comments, "Proceeds from control tend to be less conspicuous when thus divided, and no one agency increases its power to the point at which the members of the group take alarm. It does not follow, however, that diversified control does more than diversify the proceeds." [47]

If we accept Skinner's proposition that environmental reinforcement patterns largely determine behavior, we must confront the question of cultural design directly. We cannot begin at the beginning, so we must locate a departure point for rationalizing a design. Thus Skinner's definitional system, which is largely designed to avoid querying human purpose, reverts to that question. Skinner is not unaware of this circle, and he answers that survival is one bedrock value on which the human race must agree. "If a science of behavior can discover those conditions of life which make for the *ultimate strength of men,* it may provide a set of 'moral values . . .' " (italics added).[48] Survival is the evolutionist's reference point.

Skinner assumes, as do all evolutionary theorists, that survival is basic to any species including the human. Yet a political philosophy cannot rest on survival as a summary of human purpose. A more specific insight is needed to justify political obligation, the allocation of resources, and the distribution of power. Skinner does this, as was pointed out above, by referring to general a priori values. Liberal theory requires a more refined argument for its values than Skinner's common-sense starting point. We will shortly argue that Erik Erikson furnishes such a refinement in his concept of identity.

46. Robert Dahl and Charles Lindblom, *Politics, Economics, and Welfare: Planning and Politico-Economic Systems Resolved into Basic Social Processes* (New York: Harper, 1953), chapters 10 and 11, pp. 272–323.

47. Skinner, *Science and Human Behavior,* p. 441, cf. *Walden Two,* p. 273.

48. Skinner, *Science and Human Behavior,* p. 445, cf. p. 433; *Walden Two,* pp. 114–15; Kariel, "Political Relevance of Behavioral and Existentialist Psychology," pp. 336–37.

As for Skinner's environmental control argument, it needs to be pointed out that Skinner does try to deal with scientific totalitarianism. He supports diversification of social control in the period before human behavior is sufficiently understood to justify concentrating enough power to institute rational changes.[49] Skinner bravely assumes that a class of planners will emerge who will find sufficient positive reinforcement in scientific governing to immunize them against the infection of Caesarism and that they will not run away with the power engendered by monopolizing political coercion.[50]

A major limit in rationalizing social control is that, as Skinner occasionally mentions, part of the reinforcement pattern governing human behavior is inaccessible to even the most pervasive government control. Mead argues that self-growth springs primarily from interpersonal stimuli. Programming interpersonal relations increasingly engages management relations specialists and public relations advisers. Their impact is confined largely to late childhood and adulthood. Basic shaping occurs in the family, as Freud so dramatically establishes and Erikson confirms. To directly influence the style and content of infancy and childhood would require the most zealous dictatorship (or Skinner's *Walden Two*).

Since we can all doubt the imminence of enough scientifically valid knowledge of interpersonal relations to justify such an enormous extension of social control, another alternative must be found. Political theorists must construct a social-control strategy which maximizes the application of people's best knowledge while minimizing actual and potential coercion.

There is an instructive example of a partial solution in the history of economics. Socialists argue that society can be redeemed only if the government controls and manages the economic base in line with the best scientific principles. John Maynard Keynes suggested a different strategy. Keynes emphasized that the government commands a substantial proportion of society's economic transactions simply by carrying on its normal functions.

49. Skinner, *Science and Human Behavior*, p. 437 ff.
50. Skinner, *Walden Two*, pp. 251–76.

Adequate control could be acquired by manipulating those parts of the economy which the government normally effects. The government dominates fiscal and monetary controls, tax levels, spending in the economy, and even the symbolic dimensions of the economy. Total control is not necessary—only careful management of part of the equation. The government's power increases to the extent that other variables in the equation are randomized and resist organization into counter-productive pressure. Keynes's argument fits well with the traditional liberal emphasis on freedom from overt control.

The analogy to Keynes should not be carried too far, but there is a case for a Keynesian strategy in managing social transactions. The prohibition experiment illustrated the perils of imposing social reform by fiat. Government strongly influences the social fabric through hiring policies, educational systems, personnel practices, the symbolic gestures of officialdom, and the norms established for clientele relationships. Direct controls cannot be avoided, of course. Yet government's ability to coerce change is sharply limited by a scarcity of control resources. The aphoristic summary of the argument is that government should only do by force what it cannot achieve by example. Skinner's emphasis on positive reinforcement is capable of a much wider application than simply the distribution of explicit rewards for acceptable behavior. A Keynesian strategy amounts to socially reinforcing through example useful patterns of behavior. Force is justifiable only when more powerful reinforcement patterns are available to those who directly oppose some basic norm of society.

There are many examples of indirect government engineering. Nondiscrimination clauses in government contracts, racial integration of the armed services, elaborate procedures for due process in governmental dealings, public adherence by leaders to an American creed, and an emphasis on rational argument in political matters have had widespread multiplier effects in society. Corporations reconsidered discriminatory hiring practices, communities passed open housing laws, unions pressured for fair grievance procedures, and large numbers of citizens have been socialized to rationality and nonviolence in public behavior. The failures have been conspicuous, of course.

One reason liberal governments haven't been more effective in securing social change is that these strategies have rarely been used persistently. Contemporary liberalism has also suffered from a failure to justify its values coherently. The historic liberal movements in France, England, and America secured notable social improvements at times when the liberal ethic was justified by intelligible arguments. The traditional arguments have foundered as the language of justification has changed. Simultaneously, conservatism has asserted itself in the oscillation of power and undone the liberal behavioral ethic (even while incorporating liberal policy reforms).

The Limits of Skinner's System

Skinner's exploration of social control reveals the inescapability of behavioral conditioning. Environment may not be determining, but it is a major part of every life.[51] Green based his claim that government could be relatively inactive on an incautious assessment of the influence of other social institutions and an optimistic view of the individual's ability to assert his or her own self-development in a world of conflicting reinforcement patterns. Green wanted to remove the worst temptations by temperance laws and restrictions on contract. Skinner tells us enough about the phenomenon of social control to reveal the complexity of ensuring Green's positive liberty.

To distinguish positive liberty from negative liberty, we must return to the question Skinner evades: the purpose of humankind. Until it is established what people are about, there is no standard for judging what is positive and what is negative. Skinner sets up a program for finding some components of a standard when he suggests testing to see if loving one's neighbor, for example, is positively reinforcing and therefore part of what makes an individual happy.[52] Skinner, it turns out, is a utilitarian in much the same

51. Skinner, *Science and Human Behavior,* pp. 434–35.
52. Ibid., p. 429.

sense as Bentham and Mill.[53] Skinner's categories lead to the same problem Green identified in English utilitarianism: how are risk-taking and altruism to be explained? Maybe it can be argued that risking one's life for someone else is positively reinforcing though it surely violates the standard of survival on which evolutionary theory is founded.[54] To ground a political ethic on the proposition that the business of members of the species is to do only that which is positively reinforcing is ultimately to justify utilitarian anarchy.

In *Walden Two,* Skinner describes a society which agrees to certain values with their attendant behavioral restrictions. He invests behavioral science with control over members' lives.[55] Skinner escapes the anarchist implications of his utilitarian assumptions by using the time-honored device of a contract. Members agree to the regime as the price of admission. So again we are returned to the need for some values around which the community can organize. Skinner's valuation of creativity, voluntarism, security, and general happiness places him close to the liberal camp. As we hope to demonstrate, a better job can be done of justifying these values and some others that Skinner puts aside, such as liberty and equality.

The reason Skinner lacks a clear justification for the values he begins with is because he refuses to deal with the "O" in the S-O-R model. Mead argues that the organism operates through the mechanism of role-taking. In Skinner's framework, human behavior arises from a limited repertoire of behavioral responses. Skinner is on solid ground in claiming that human responses undergo extensive modification and selective reinforcement. That may be; however, behavior is not infinitely plastic, as Skinner realizes.[56] People

53. Skinner does dissent from the "greatest happiness" principle of classical utilitarianism, but only on the grounds that the principle conceals the difficulty of specifying the component variables. See *Science and Human Behavior,* p. 329.
54. See Skinner's argument on suicide, *ibid.,* p. 223.
55. Skinner, *Walden Two,* pp. 174–75.
56. Skinner, *Science and Human Behavior,* p. 56; cf. p. 93, 145–48. See Mead's comment on the content of the "O," in *Mind, Self, and Society,* p. 141n.

actively rearrange nature's reinforcement patterns in structures which demonstrate regularity over time. The fact that this happens indicates that there is something in the organism enabling it to separate itself from the physical environment.

Skinner runs into trouble dismissing the organism when he tries to discuss the transference phenomenon (which he defines as induction). Experiments demonstrate that reinforcement aimed at stimulating one form of behavior often leads to greater efficiency in other kinds of behavior. He explains this by discussing the complexity of separating out stimulus and response and the interrelations between them.[57] The point is, as Skinner concedes, "The behavior with which we are usually concerned, from either a theoretical or practical point of view, is continuously modified from a basic material which is largely undifferentiated." [58] For this reason, he prefers to talk about deprivation-satiation, for example, rather than instincts.[59] Skinner's system requires a materialist hypothesis if it is to be carried to its logical conclusion. But as Joseph Church points out:

> The problem here is of who or what it is that thinks. It seems quite clear that it is not nervous systems or language or response sets or schemata that think, but organisms. . . . environmental events do not automatically evoke symbolic formulations or problem solutions, except when these have already been worked out and are available as habits—habits, let it be stressed, of a very general kind, since it is not particular neuromuscular sequences or even particular acts that are habitual, but kinds of activity.[60]

Mead is probably right in theorizing that social behavior arises largely from habits formulated through role-taking. Skinner gives us little help in finding out where these habits originate and *why* they have the content they do. All he can suggest is that some habits are functional for survival and others are not.

57. Skinner, *Science and Human Behavior,* pp. 129–40.
58. *Ibid.,* p. 93.
59. *Ibid.,* pp. 145–48.
60. Joseph Church, *Language and the Discovery of Reality: A Developmental Psychology of Cognition* (New York: Random House, 1961), p. 157, cf. pp. 209–15.

In the final analysis, individuals are called upon to structure their environment in advance of precise knowledge of the consequences of actions. People create their habits through group interaction. Skinner's research may tell us what operant behavior individuals demonstrate at some specific moment—but what is the tendency or direction of habit patterns over time? [61] To address that question, we need to probe the human organism much more deeply than Skinner's system of categories permits. We need generalizations about the directionality of the organism which go beyond a counting up of operant characteristics. These generalizations cannot be formulated without abstracting from the physical evidence.

Survival as an explanation of human purpose carries the same limitations as Mead's "social adjustment" and Freud's "normality." All three are explanations which support a few normative propositions like: people ought not to kill each other; individuals ought to operate on a basis of mutual respect; the range of experience available to members of a society should contain at least a few alternatives; and so on. These are the beginnings of a new argument for liberation, but there is still not enough structure in these explanations to answer the tough questions of allocation of resources, obligation, and the control of power. The urgency of these questions is heightened by Skinner's perceptive analysis of social control, but the resolution of them is not greatly aided by promising simple utilitarianism as an explanation of human purpose.

Conclusion

This chapter began with an enumeration of three central problems in the legacy of Freudianism: (1) an unsatisfactory theory of human mutuality, (2) a negative account of social control functions, and (3) an incomplete theory of the life cycle with its implications for human purpose. I have tried to show how Mead establishes a basis for a theory of mutuality by his discussion of role-taking.

61. George Homans, *The Human Group* (New York: Harcourt, 1950), p. 176.

Skinner analyzes the phenomenon of social control and suggests a framework for nonpunitive methods of reform. Both theorists place human behavior in a broader perspective than Freud and establish the need for a more comprehensive theory of the life cycle. At the same time, neither Mead nor Skinner provides an explanation of human purpose sufficient to the consummation of a justification for the values fundamental to human liberation.

chapter five

The Natural Self

Assumptions about human purpose are the bedrock of all philosophy. However, much philosophy concerns purposes we would like to ascribe to human nature rather than purposes which can be observed in the reality of behavior. Jefferson ennobled human nature by assuming purpose could be found in the implications of humanity's creation by God. Inspiring as that possibility is, Jefferson was among the very first and foremost in the struggle to protect individuals against other individuals—he was the author of much of our civil liberties system.

The utilitarians saw a kind of purpose in the pursuit of happiness, a formulation which had the force of simplicity. However, utilitarianism in practice led to the miseries of a raw industrial society. It became increasingly obvious that utilitarianism provided a framework for exploitation because it never came to grips with exactly what happiness consists of. Thus, the happiness of the avaricious entrepreneur came out equal on the scales of justice with the supposed happiness of the child who was free to take a job in a spinning mill.

The problem for contemporary liberals is to find a specification of purpose-in-fact rather than ideal-purpose. And this leads us straight to scientifically oriented students of human nature. Freud's *normality,* Mead's *adjustment,* and Skinner's *survival* are all approximations to a statement of human purpose. Yet each, while simple, does not afford the detail of prescription that a powerful political concept requires. What is normal? Adjustment to which standard of relationships? Whose survival? Each of these three psychological theories is inadequate to the task of constructing a politics of liberation. At the same time, each of the three provides compelling evidence, first, that people are individually adaptive though tied inextricably to society and, second, that substantial social conditioning is inevitable.

Erik Erikson tells us that the formation of an *identity* is the purpose-in-fact of human behavior. It is about the project of identity that behavior gathers. Our agenda must then be: What is Erikson's identity theory? Does it fit with substantial evidence concerning political behavior? What are its implications for political thought? To spare the tedium of tripartite development, we shall discuss these three questions in the context, once again, of an issue: the relationship of individual to community, the unsolved question of liberalism.

Erik Erikson remarked recently that liberals have no theory of childhood. A comment like that invites a question: Why should they?

In our inherited liberal tradition, one gets the overwhelming sense that individuals are viewed as standard adult units isolated from others by competing claims for scarce gratifications. Yet it is quite obvious on a moment's introspection that we all have histories. These histories have rhythms which are largely derived from the communities we are part of. Yet each history is differentiated by the way we live with or against those rhythms. Communities are formed around the producing and sustaining of children, adults, and old people. Thus childhood and the remnants of childhood in adulthood are most significant.

It is too easy to take from Erikson's remark about liberals and childhood, let it be noted, a return to the Oedipus complex and the familiar reductionism of Freudian psychoanalysis. What I will attempt to show is how Erikson has told us something of the rhythm of our natures and the correlative harmonies and disharmonies of our communities. I will end up writing of the *natural* person in the sense of potentiality in human nature, not in the sense of surface behavior. *Natural,* in this context, will become a normative as well as a descriptive term.

We are searching for that model of personal development in which the potentialities of human nature for self and social realization are most likely to be realized. It is to this model that political theory must direct itself. We shall see that, by the very nature of our findings, relatively little can be done to enforce any model of development on specific individuals. On the other hand, a great deal can be done to so order the state and society to enable such a self-development in the largest possible number of people. If the principal conditions for human development can be located, the task of defining positive liberty or, better, a politics of liberation will be manageable.

The inquiry begins with a bit of history. Erikson is a Freudian and the first step must be to establish that continuity.[1]

The Origin of Identity

In the the 1920s and 1930s Freud developed a more comprehensive theory of the ego than in his earlier work which emphasized the id. *The Ego and the Id* (1923) and *The Problem of Anxiety* (1926) are the major works, though he continued to elaborate themes relating to ego psychology until his death. Anna Freud expanded her father's insights, and she was joined late in the 1930s by two major figures: Heinz Hartmann and Erik Erikson. Both Hartmann and Erikson are important to the history of psychoanalysis, though the two theories have not yet been integrated,

1. Erik Erikson retired in 1970 from Harvard University where he was Professor of Human Development; he continues to do research, write, and lecture. Robert Coles's intimate study, *Erik H. Erikson: The Growth of His Work* (Boston: Little, Brown, 1970), details Erikson's personal background and the formation of his ideas in relation to his major writings. A condensed version of the last two chapters of the present work was presented to the American Political Science Association Convention Symposium on Transactionalism, September, 1972.

and Erikson's, unlike Hartmann's, extends to social and political implications.[2] As we have seen (in Wolin), the significance of Freud is that, while liberalism factored out the soul by its materialist preoccupation, Freud factored it back in again, transformed into id, superego, and most important, ego.

Freud commented in 1923 that "As a frontier-creature, the ego tries to mediate between the world and the id, to make the id pliable to the world and, by means of its muscular activity, to make the world fall in with the wishes of the id." [3] The ego is the device which contends with three crucial forces: instincts, conscience, and the external world. To the extent that Freud's earlier work implied the supremacy of the id, it did not satisfactorily explain the impact of either conscience or the external world. Freud, as we noted earlier, struggled with a "reality-principle" to explain the relation of instinct to social life, but his theory remains inadequate the essential question of people's social relations.[4]

Anna Freud's contribution to the unfolding of ego psychology is an analysis of the ego's defensive functions. Her clinical research detailed the emergence of ego defenses as the self struggles with internal and external pressures. These defensive phenomena sometimes become permanently ingrained in one's character.[5] The major implication of her work is that the ego is an independent force which may, in fact, come to dominate the id.

2. The historical material on ego psychology is based largely on David Rapaport, "A Historical Survey of Psychoanalytic Ego Psychology," an introduction to "Identity and the Life Cycle," by Erikson, *Psychological Issues,* Vol. I (1959) p. 1, Monograph 1 (New York: International Universities Press), pp. 5–17. The development of an independent ego psychology is anticipated by Freud in 1905, *Works,* Vol. 7, p. 162; cf. Vol. 19, pp. 17, 24. See also Heinz Hartmann, *Essays on Ego Psychology* (New York: International Universities Press, 1964), pp. xii–xiii; Erik Erikson, *Insight and Responsibility* (New York: Norton, 1964), pp. 31–33; and Alan Wheelis, *The Quest for Identity* (New York: Norton, 1958), pp. 75–76.

3. Sigmund Freud, *Works,* Vol. 19, p. 56, cf. p. 26; Anna Freud, *The Ego and the Mechanisms of Defense* (New York: International Universities Press, 1966), p. 176.

4. Freud, *Works,* Vol. 19, p. 55.

5. Anna Freud, *The Ego and the Mechanisms of Defense,* Ch. 3, pp. 28–41; Ch. 4, pp. 42–53.

If it is true that the ego emerges as the preeminent force in normal human behavior, then we begin to see a key to the riddle of human nature. Some theorists would let it go at that—arguing that the ego does triumph and that the ego can be socialized to love and harmony. But that stretches things considerably. While the ego may grow in power, Freudian theory offers no basis for assuming that the id and the superego simply fade away or even that they always lose in the continual contest of the self. Freud characteristically writes in terms of images of dynamic forces in struggle. He makes explicit some of the typical patterns of struggle, especially in childhood. Erikson continues Freud's basic design, but forges ahead into the patterns to be found in adolescence, adulthood, and old age. With bold vision informed by a variety of observation and experimentation, Erikson presents a theory of life as a cycle of events in the personality. In working through these events, individuals write the story of their lives. And it is through understanding the pattern of these events that societies and institutions become harmful or useful, frustrating or liberating.

A student of both Sigmund and Anna Freud, Erikson refused to accept "the oedipus trinity as an irreducible schema for man's irrational conduct." [6] Erikson was intrigued by Freud's image of mind struggling with body. He began to look for some way to characterize the meaning or direction of the whole pattern of struggle. Rather than rejecting the instinctual research of Freud, Erikson incorporated it into a subtler and more comprehensive theory of the human life cycle. Ultimately, Erikson arrived at the concept of "identity" as a *name* for the ego's integrative function.[7]

Erikson conceptualizes the human organisms as a *process* rather than as a *thing*.[8] The burden of his effort is to understand natural patterns of adaptivity in the human organism. He reinterprets Freud's id-ego-superego as a trilogy of processes which "exist by

6. Erikson, "Identity and the Life Cycle," p. 21.
7. See Erikson, *Identity: Youth and Crisis* (New York: Norton, 1968), pp. 218–19; *Insight and Responsibility*, pp. 147–49; and his reinterpretation of Freudian dream theory, *ibid.*, pp. 198–200.
8. Erikson, *Childhood and Society*, 2d ed. (New York: Norton, 1963), p. 34.

and are relative to each other." In Erikson's modification of Freudian categories, the *id* refers to the body-oriented (organ mode) life functions. Any theory of the life cycle must look to what is inescapably regular in human experience. We all have bodies of uniform developmental characteristics. Changes in the body present the self with challenges of vast consequences for relationships with the social environment. Equally obvious is the fact that people do not simply act out body-oriented functions. Something intervenes and introduces organization to the impulsive appetites of the body. This is the *ego*. The ego must act in a context of external as well as internal pressures. Society limits and shapes the possibilities of expression and is in turn shaped by them. For this process of "the social organization of ego organisms," Erikson uses Freud's term, the *superego*.[9] Erikson's theory of the life cycle attempts to integrate these three processes and the major events of their interaction.

Out of a lifetime of research and clinical observation in a wide variety of settings, Erikson comes to the conclusion that there are eight stages to the human life cycle, each with its roots in a major phase of biological development. The early stages follow Freud's model. The infant struggles through a series of sharp changes: from total dependence, to the beginnings of self-control of bodily functions, to the shocks of accelerating independence. Each of these phases is prompted by changes in the genital and muscular development of the organism. Linked inextricably to these developments are modes of behavior: the child who has just learned to move about (Stage III) becomes for a while an explorer, poking around, getting into things, testing the boundaries of a suddenly much wider physical universe. Erikson calls this stage the "locomotor genital" organ mode. The behavior it gives rise to may be described as intrusive and aggressive.

Organ-mode behavior constitutes one coordinate of human development. A second coordinate is the response such behavior meets in the environment. Cultures can be revealingly described according to the rituals and practices by which they cope with each

9. Erikson, "Identity and the Life Cycle," p. 48.

stage of development. Some build fences around a child of this age, others try to create environments of interesting objects. It is uniformly necessary, however, for all cultural practices to impose limits on the universe of a mobile child who is, nevertheless, quite defenseless against the dangers of some objects and some people. It is against these limits that the child encounters conditioning, rebuff, and even rejection. The specific form of intrusive aggressive behavior, influenced at this stage both by locomotor development and genital impulses, evokes particularly sensitive kinds of responses from the environment.

So we have two elements of the triad of development in place: organ-mode behavior and environmental responses. The content of these two creates the challenge for the third: What happens inside the self as it works through such a problem? How does the mind cope with each stage? More to the point, what is it that the mind must come to know to enable it to meet the next alteration in body and environment? How, in short, does each developmental stage build toward the next?

Erikson's theory about the third stage is that the mind must deal with a diad of mental sensitivities: initiative and guilt. The child needs to acquire both a general sense of initiative, of purposeful and fulfilling competencies, as well as a capacity to deal with occasional feelings of guilt over the impulse rejected by environmental limits. If that accomplishment can be consolidated in childhood, the individual will have acquired a strength useful to later challenges. A pathology of the third stage is the child so overridden by guilt feelings that the world comes to be a forbidding, naysaying, hostile place in which the promptings of self become painful and the mind despairing.

To rehearse eight stages of development and to characterize each triangle of organ-mode, environmental response, and ego challenge is a task better left to Erikson, who writes masterfully. Fortunately, we can capture the structure of his theory through a chart he originated (reproduced on p. 114).[10]

10. Erikson, *Identity*, pp. 94–95; see also discussion in *Childhood and Society*, pp. 247–74.

In Erikson's chart, the *vertical* column denotes the stages of organ-mode growth. The individual passes through eight identifiable stages beginning with the oral sensory organ-mode of the infant and culminating in physical maturity. The context of each stage is influenced primarily by genital-muscular development. Thus, using Stage II as an example, we find that the infant experiences the psycho-physical problem of toilet training (retention-elimination) attended by severe behavioral sanctions from parents. In the next development, the muscular and sexual development of the locomotor-genital stage manifests itself through intrusive, aggressive behavior, which in turn meets with a different set of responses in the environment.

The *horizontal* row apportions the series of time spaces in which the culture deals with each organ-mode stage through its conventions and customs. These stages have no standard names and vary somewhat with the patterns of child care, ritual, and social-sexual behavior in different cultures.

The *diagonal,* which is the object of the chart, indicates the ego functions confronted at each stage; for example, the intrusive aggressive behavior of the locomotor-genital stage in confrontation with social discipline leads to a conflict between "initiative and guilt."

Each individual stage of growth has its precursors and after-effects. Erikson has suggested a number of these in relation to the fifth stage of development. (See the boxes *off* the diagonal.)

The natural society would organize a series of developmental arrangements corresponding with the differing epigenetic stages and supporting the favorable resolution of the dichotomies faced by the ego. Erikson, of course, realizes the tentativeness of such charting. The significance of it is in the implication that the individual, influenced by his physiological development, faces the ego task of reconciling personal development with the materials available in the society.[11]

Erikson's theory deviates from Freud's in the crucial respect that human instincts are not considered to be controlling in the reduc-

11. Erikson, *Childhood and Society,* p. 270.

Erikson's Chart of Epigenetic Human Development

Organ-Mode Stages		1	2	3	4	5	6	7	8
Maturity	VIII								INTEGRITY vs. DESPAIR
Adulthood	VII							GENERATIVITY vs. STAGNATION	
Young Adulthood	VI						INTIMACY vs. ISOLATION		
Puberty and Adolescence	V	Temporal Perspective vs. Time Confusion	Self-Certainty vs. Self-Consciousness	Role Experimentation vs. Role Fixation	Apprenticeship vs. Work Paralysis	IDENTITY vs. IDENTITY CONFUSION	Sexual Polarization vs. Bisexual Confusion	Leader- and Followership vs. Authority Confusion	Ideological Commitment vs. Confusion of Values
Latency	IV				INDUSTRY vs. INFERIORITY	Task Identification vs. Sense of Futility			
Locomotor-Genital	III			INITIATIVE vs. GUILT		Anticipation of Roles vs. Role Inhibition			
Muscular-Anal	II		AUTONOMY vs. SHAME, DOUBT			Will to Be Oneself vs. Self-Doubt			
Oral-Sensory	I	TRUST vs. MISTRUST				Mutual Recognition vs. Autistic Isolation			

Phases of Cultural Responses

tionist sense. Erikson argues that "the drives man is born with are not instincts," because they do not "carry in themselves the patterns of completion, of self-preservation, of interaction with any segment of nature; tradition and conscience must organize them." [12] Erikson places the maxim that "man is a social creature" in a more sophisticated perspective by relating the individual's experience to a complex of physical, social, and adaptive factors.[13]

Erikson is clearly *not* telling us that we are *self*-acting autonomously in an environment. Our biology and our culture are far too important for that. The vertical and horizontal coordinates of his chart are meant only to describe the matrix of our existence, not the simplicity of an *inter*action between body and culture. Rather we are *trans*acting creatures, living on a tentative diagonal, synthesizing or fragmenting a set of forces, none of which are independent of the others, and all of which are keyed to the rhythm of birth, growth, aging, and death.[14] We have in the epigenetic chart a kind of place-map of the larger transactional frame of our

12. *Ibid.,* p. 95; Erik Erikson, *Gandhi's Truth* (New York: Norton, 1969), p. 427.

13. See Freud's speculations about development, *Works,* Vol. 19, p. 29; Anna Freud's discussion in *The Ego and the Mechanisms of Defense,* Ch. 5, pp. 54–65; Carl Jung, *Modern Man in Search of a Soul* (New York: Harcourt, 1933), p. 58; Harold Lasswell's character types based on unresolved developmental conflicts in his *Power and Personality* (New York: Norton, 1948), pp. 38–39, 61; Joseph Church on "growth ambivalence" in *Language and the Discovery of Reality: A Developmental Psychology of Cognition* (New York: Random House, 1961), p. 205; and Robert Lane on need-fulfillment through political ideas, *Political Thinking and Consciousness* (Chicago: Markham, 1969), pp. 7–23.

14. See John Dewey and Arthur Bentley, *Knowing and the Known* (Boston: Beacon Press, 1949), p. 108; pp. 120–21 for a negative test of the fit of identity with the transactional framework; p. 130 for their treatment of "psyche"; p. 138 for their discussion of organism as a collection of transactions; and p. 104 for a review of the relationship between the natural and the transactional.

NOTE: The basic chart reproduced on the facing page appears in *Identity: Youth and Crisis* (1968), p. 94 (used by permission of W. W. Norton and Co.). I have added the names (Maturity, etc.) given to the "Organ-Mode Stages" by Erikson in a less complete form of the chart in *Childhood and Society* (2d Ed., 1963), p. 273. The titles "Organ-Mode Stages" and "Phases of Cultural Responses" have also been added by me.

existence. It is in the consistency of the patterns of transactional events that we begin to find those "knowings" which permit self-understanding and maybe a bit of provisional self and social mastery.

Whether or not one accepts Erikson's tentative conclusions about the structure of life stages, the central discovery of his theory may be valid: the function of identity in human life. Identity formation and defense is the common theme linking all eight stages. The development of the ego through all its trials finds a theme in the identity concept. What does that mean?

Erikson describes the identity concept as follows:

> The ego, if understood as a central and partially unconscious organizing agency, must at any given stage of life deal with a changing Self which demands to be synthesized with abandoned and anticipated selves. This suggestion would be applicable to the body ego, which could be said to be that part of the Self provided by the experience of one's body and, therefore, might more appropriately be called the *body self*. It concerns the ego ideal as the representative of the ideas, images, and configurations which serve the persistent comparison with an *ideal self*. It, finally, would apply to part of what I have called ego identity, namely, that part which consists of role images. What could consequently be called the *self-identity* emerges from experiences in which temporarily confused selves are successfully reintegrated in an ensemble of roles which also secure social recognition.[15]

Identity, in short, refers to the ego's attempt to integrate instinct, reality, and the ideal as a means of finding a place for the self in society.

Identity is essentially a sense of who we are which emerges from a mutual recognition between the self and others in a cultural environment. Retreating for a moment from the close analysis Erik-

---

15. Erikson, *Identity*, p. 211. Cf. *Childhood and Society*, p. 262, and Heinz Hartmann's "conflict-free" ego sphere, in his *Ego Psychology and the Problem of Adaptation* (New York: International Universities Press, 1958), pp. 8–9.

son invites us to, we can see life generally as a matter of action in the face of uncertainty. Our bodies keep changing; the fixities people create in the form of jobs and status are always fragile; relationships with others are usually complex. That is the challenge of being human. The human repertoire of possible responses to uncertainty is vastly amplified through the power of a highly developed mind capable of imagination, planning, and comparing, as well as error, miscalculation, and downright stupidity. The most ingenious of these responses is the creation of an identity. An identity enables the self both to avoid dealing with every situation as a novelty and to create a locus in a social environment such that incoming cues and stimuli can be structured and rendered manageable. Our self-image serves as the vehicle of social transactions. Identity formation helps keep life's uncertainties at bay by creating an island of semi-certainty. Erikson summarizes the reasons why the formation of an identity becomes the major project of human life:

> this central process guards the coherence and the individuality of experience by gearing the individual for shocks threatening from sudden discontinuities in the organism as well as in the milieu; by enabling it to anticipate inner as well as outer dangers; and by integrating endowment and social opportunities. It thus assures to the individual a sense of coherent individuation and identity: of being one's self, of being all right, and of being on the way to becoming what other people, at their kindest, take one to be.[16]

The preceding discussion would be a sterile exercise in nomenclature were it not for the fact that Erikson has detailed some of the workings of identity formation in his clinically based writings. Identity formation and defense is a lifelong process, though it reaches a specific crisis in late adolescence (see chart above). What happens in adolescence? As Erikson puts it, this is "a time of life when the body changes its proportions radically, when genital puberty floods body and imagination with all manner of impulses,

16. Erikson, *Childhood and Society,* p. 35.

when intimacy with the other sex approaches and is, on occasion, forced on the young person, and when the immediate future confronts one with too many conflicting possibilities and choices." [17] Adolescence, at least as I remember it, is a rather bizarre, messy, exhilarating time of life. Cultural responses to adolescence vary considerably. The adolescent, partially independent of the boundaries of home life, emerges into his environment with much of the panoply of adulthood—cars, some skills, high octane amusements, weapons perhaps, aptitudes, and physical completeness. No wonder adults in the environment respond in so many diverse ways— from D.A.R. awards for good citizenship to armored police units for protesters and dissenters who take their citizenship a little too seriously; from well-chaperoned high school proms to well-concealed fantasies of teenage orgies.

It is a time of great uncertainty. This is the hour of the identity crisis or maybe the identity test. The personality gathers its strengths acquired from previous developments, reckons with its weaknesses, and tries to struggle through to some settlement with the social environment. Not that one is certified as a plumber or printer or professor by the age of 19 or 22, but more that one is seen to be inclined toward some kind of definable personality tending toward some self-suited vocational possibilities.

The opposite end of the scale from identity achievement is identity confusion. Everyone learns to live with some identity confusion. Sometimes we positively enjoy it, but that's because we can afford to, knowing that there is a safe sideline to which to retire if the game gets rough. Erikson suggests that the optimum development from this stage is a sense of identity authentic in terms of a personal past, a generally understood present, and a likely future. Fencing with confusion is a normal part of the match. In fact, it might be said that people mold an identity from all of the confusing possibilities in their surroundings.

Is there such a thing as too much identity too early? Answer: of course. The child rigidly programmed into adolescence as a particular something comes out with an identity all right, but one

17. *Identity,* p. 132–33, p. 246.

which is not very likely to survive the currents and tides of experience. So identity represents the creative device by which individuals negotiate their way in the world. That takes a certain toughness which comes only with the tempering of real experience.

While the identity test is formative in adolescence, the identity created must be viable for a future structured by physical maturation and the implications of mortality. With a little luck, the adult has achieved some kind of workable identity, some sort of arrangement with reality which permits a relatively functional lifestyle and a few pleasures of expression. Physical development reaches its peak, and the reminders of time's inevitable course direct the mind's eye to the meaning of the past as a text for the present. The tension which occurs here is between "generativity and stagnation." By generativity, Erikson means a sense that we have made something of our lives. The adult test of "generativity" is a kind of retrospective identity crisis. We may have made something like a building, a book, or a revolution. We may have perfected a competency. We may have made someone in our own image to carry on that something we think we are making—a child, a student, a congregation. A sense of stagnation attends the feeling of having made little that is enduring or meaningful.

Identity is a transactional process between the individual and society by which both, in a sense, are created and recreated. Adult society characteristically revolves around the question of life work and expressive activity. Personal reputation becomes a vital concern. As Parsons, Bales, and Shils point out, the achievement of competence in socially favored roles creates a transferability of status. To serve society is to serve self.[18] Some identities have significant self-reinforcing, and even historic, impact on the cultural environment.

18. Cited in Sidney Verba, *Small Groups and Political Behavior* (Princeton, N.J.: Princeton University Press, 1961), pp. 126–27. George Homans comments that "If we examine the motives we usually call self-interest, we shall find that they are, for the most part, neither individual nor selfish but that they are the product of group life and serve the ends of a whole group not just an individual." *The Human Group* (New York: Harcourt, 1950), pp. 95–96.

The thesis of Erikson's psycho-historical classic, *Young Man Luther,* is that the resolution of an individual identity crisis in unique cultural circumstances can have enormous consequences for history. Luther's rebellion against a particularly strong-willed German father became Luther's revolution against an authoritarian Catholic church. The symmetry of Luther's personal rebelliousness and the feelings of the mass of Germans in the sixteenth century sparked a cultural explosion which Luther certainly didn't anticipate and was hardly able to control. The process of civilization, according to Erikson, does far more in the typical case to mold specific individuals than the reverse. Yet it is personal agency that synthesizes instinct and conditioning.

Erikson's theory combines insights from Freud's organically based psychoanalysis, Mead's role theory, and Skinner's concepts of conditioned behavior. Some of the strongest conditioners of identity formation are the roles (identity materials) available in the environment. The working out of identity is almost by definition a process of acquiring and relating roles played by others in relation to the self. Erikson's research on child rearing supports the claim in *Childhood and Society* that parental practices concerning psycho-sexual development exert an exceedingly powerful conditioning influence on the identity formation of individuals. Were Skinner's utopia, *Walden Two,* established today, it is predictable that many of the initial assumptions about child rearing would be based on Erikson's work.

A *caveat* needs to be entered here. Erikson notes that identity formation and defense remain largely unconscious. To the extent that the process becomes conscious (voluntarily or involuntarily) it is likely to be painful.[19] Erikson fears the kind of pop culture uses to which identity theory is put. The forces converging on the ego are powerful and only partly manipulable. The mind ingeniously anaesthetizes consciousness to many of the struggles living entails. The margin of consciousness which can be deployed to enrich and diversify experience is too precious to squander in tan-

19. Erikson, *Identity,* pp. 22–23, 28–29, See pp. 300, 314–15 for Erikson's reaction to the self-proclaimed identity crisis of contemporary youth.

gling with the whole range of inner conflicts. Pop psychology damages understanding when its purveyors pretend that answers exist for every internal discontent. Challenges and conflicts are the stuff of individual life. Without them, we would be condemned to a bovine, banal existence.

Erikson's identity concept will seem ambiguous to the operations-oriented researcher, though psychoanalysts now commonly apply the concept in therapy. The contribution of Erikson's formulation is that it narrows the ambiguity and specifies some of the mechanics which account for the patterns of individual activity.[20]

Before we can move directly to politics, several important issues related to the identity concept need to be examined: the phenomenon of negative and positive identity, the development of collective identity, the relationship of identity formation to personal and social change, and finally, again, the uses of identity as a statement of purpose-in-fact.

The principal therapeutic use of the identity concept is to investigate neurosis stemming from identity confusion. Erikson realized that identity formation is not straightforward—there is often a dialectic between positive and negative identities "composed of what he [the individual] has been shamed for, what he has been punished for, and what he feels guilty about: his failures in competency and goodness." The specific content of negative identities may originate in observations of people interesting to the individual whom he dislikes or is taught to condemn, e.g., a derelict uncle. "Identity means an integration of all previous identifications and self-images, including the negative onces." [21] Schizophrenia is often a failure to integrate positive and negative identities.

Erikson's duality of positive and negative identities makes coherent the earlier Freudian discussion of reaction formations, repression, and projection. As Anna Freud suggested, these are primarily *defensive* mechanisms of the Ego.[22] The objects of defen-

20. For Erikson's comment on the ambiguity of the concept, see *Identity,* p. 208.

21. Erik Erikson and Richard Evans, *Dialogue with Erik Erikson* (New York: Dutton, 1967), p. 36. See also Erikson, *Identity,* p. 203.

22. Anna Freud, *The Ego and the Mechanisms of Defense,* pp. 73–74.

sive ego activities are, following Erikson, negative identifications. Culture largely determines the materials available for identity formation. A culture may create for groups within it only negative identity materials. Erikson illustrated the point in 1950 in regard to the problem of black identity: "Three [negative] identities are formed: (1) mammy's oral-sensual 'honey-child'—tender, expressive, rhythmical; (2) the evil identity of the dirty, anal-sadistic, phallic-rapist 'nigger'; and (3) the clean, anal-compulsive, restrained, friendly, but always sad 'white man's Negro.' " [23] Erikson found a similar pattern in research on the Sioux Indians. What makes these identity materials *negative* is that they are preferred by the dominant cultural group with a patronizing, condemnatory attitude. The transaction serves to prop up the chauvinism of the master group. Sadly, its victims occasionally yield to the force of convention and accept the roles proffered so to survive a hostile environment.

For this reason, concessions to one's negative identity engender self-hate. The feeling of being outside the culture's accepted identity structure or of occupying its bottom rungs is noted by David Apter in *Ideology and Discontent,* "For the truly superfluous men, there is no ideology, only generalized hatred. Speed, violence, a frenetic round of petulant actions, or perhaps more simply despair, characterize these groups, which have been largely ignored by a prosperous society." [24] Erikson suggests that this feeling, which is often intensified in the identity-crisis of youth, accounts for the more irrational manifestations of anarchic and radical attitudes.[25] On the other hand, the success of one's positive identity generates feelings of self-mastery and ego gratification.[26] The "black is beautiful" movement captures the meaning of power over one's own cultural role-structure.

23. Erikson, *Childhood and Society,* p. 242.
24. David Apter, ed., *Ideology and Discontent* (New York: Free Press, 1964), pp. 38–39.
25. Erikson, *Identity,* p. 189. For an illustration of "negative identity" see Erikson, *Young Man Luther* (New York: Norton, 1958), p. 219; Erikson, *Gandhi's Truth,* p. 434.
26. Erikson, *Young Man Luther,* p. 217.

Erikson's epistemological position is closer to the idealist position than the materialist. Like Freud and Mead, Hartmann and Erikson argue that individuals construct their worlds through mental activity.[27] The self is not determined by material sense impressions. Thinking is an experimental activity for identity testing and consolidation.[28] In ego psychology, physiological drives are seen to be a major (but not entirely controlling) factor in self-development.[29] The very term identity incorporates the idea that the mind is capable of complex perceptions of time and continuity which the materialist would be hard put to explain.[30]

Another argument for this version of the idealist position is Murray Edelman's explanation of the function of symbolization, which Erikson's theory supports. One's concept of self-identity is necessarily an abstraction from the discrete events in reality. The basic technique of human abstraction is symbolization. The distortion introduced in symbolization can be systematically explained by reference to individual identity needs and group role-taking.[31] Erikson's research on identity supports the idealist epistemological argument, but in a behavioral context in that his theory gives structure to important observations about the uses and misuses of the process of human learning and communication.

In the transaction of identity formation, social ideologies are powerful—the more powerful they are to an individual, the less that person is able to make sense out of his or her own life. Erikson's analysis of ideology is worth quoting at some length. Characterizing ideology as "that system of ideals which societies present to the young," Erikson describes the functions ideology potentially serves by offering youth:

27. See Dewey and Bentley, *Knowing and the Known,* pp. 166–76 for a discussion of epistemological issues.
28. See Erikson, *Identity,* p. 220; Hartmann, *Ego Psychology,* pp. 58–60, on his views and Freud's.
29. Hartmann, *Ego Psychology,* pp. 14, 56.
30. Erikson, *Identity,* pp. 187–88; Hartmann, *Ego Psychology,* p. 43.
31. Murray Edelman, *The Symbolic Uses of Politics* (Urbana: University sity of Illinois Press, 1964) and *Politics As Symbolic Action: Mass Arousal and Quiescence* (Chicago: Markham, 1971).

(1) A simplified perspective of the future which encompasses all foreseeable time and thus counteracts individual "time confusion"; (2) some strongly felt correspondence between the inner world of ideals and evils and the social world with its goals and dangers; (3) an opportunity for exhibiting some uniformity of appearance and behavior counteracting individual identity-consciousness; (4) inducement to a collective experimentation with roles and techniques which help overcome a sense of inhibition and personal guilt; (5) introduction into the ethos of the prevailing technology and thus into sanctioned and regulated competition; (6) a geographic-historical world image as a framework for the young individual's budding identity; (7) a rationale for a sexual way of life compatible with a convincing system of principles; and (8) submission to leaders who as super-human figures or "big brothers" are above the ambivalence of the parent-child relation.[32]

Erikson's clinical research indicates substantial evidence for a functional view of ideology. His findings are congruent with those of major studies by psychologists and political scientists of the same phenomena.[33]

The function of ideology varies with psycho-sexual growth stages. In childhood, the presentation of a mythology of social

32. Erikson, *Identity*, pp. 187–88; see also "Identity and the Life Cycle," p. 23.

33. For analogies and illustrations of Erikson's view of ideology, see Heinz Hartmann on ego failure as a prelude to turning inward in search of organizing ideas, *Ego Psychology*, p. 71; Ernst Cassirer on the conditions for the recurrence of myth, in *The Myth and the State* (New Haven: Yale University Press, 1946), p. 43; Harold Lasswell on positive democratic action through shared values, *Power and Personality*, p. 188; David Apter on social and individual functions of ideology, *Ideology and Discontent*, p. 18; Robert Nisbet on alienation from community, *Community and Power* (New York: Oxford University Press, 1962), Preface; Karl Mannheim on the Marxist view of the function of political thought, *Ideology and Utopia* (New York: Harcourt, 1936), pp. 125–26; Norman Brown on the functional relation of Protestantism to Luther's time, *Life against Death* (New York: Vintage, 1959), pp. 397–99; Philip Rieff on a comparison of the psychological dimensions of the Oriental, communist, and Western ideologies, *The Triumph of the Therapeutic* (New York: Harper, 1966), pp. 19–21, 52, 70; Carl Hovland, Irving Janis, and Harold Kelley on the relations between low self-esteem and high persuadability in *Communication and Persuasion* (New Haven: Yale University Press, 1953), pp. 187–92;

heroes offers positive identity fragments.[34] A repertoire of socially accepted positive and negative identities supplies reference points for the developing youth.[35] In late adolescence, the hour of the identity crisis, Erikson points out that, "At no other time . . . does the individual feel so exposed to anarchic manifestations of his drives; at no other time does he so need oversystematised thoughts and overvalued words to give a semblance of order to his inner world." [36] Faced with the inner chaos of sexual conflict, the youth is reassured by ideologies which organize the world and reify vague anticipations of invasion and persecution.[37]

A certain framework of ideology is crucial to the developing youth, but an excess of ideology in the form of totalism is a neurotic recourse of the psychologically confused adult. Totalism refers to a forsaking of the self in a complete commitment to an externally formed system of ideas and prescriptions. A totalistic *Gestalt* becomes a way of imposing absolute boundaries where the individual lacks the inner resources to cope with reality.[38] Totalism is an ancient and much practiced recourse in periods of individual and cultural confusion. The leading recent example must, of course, be Hitler's Nazi Germany arising from the economic and psychological ruins of the First World War and the depression. Echoes of the phenomenon are traced in Ernst Cassirer's classic, *The Myth of the State*.[39]

The term identity implies continuity in the face of change. Totalism is part of the pathology of identity formation. The prob-

and the reverse phenomenon in Robert Lane, *Political Ideology: Why the American Common Man Believes What He Does* (New York: Free Press, 1962), p. 382, as well as the tenacity with which less privileged individuals will elaborate and maintain a quasi-ideological explanation of their situation, p. 73; and Lane's discussion of need fulfillment through ideology, *Political Thinking and Consciousness*, esp. pp. 17–23.
    34. Erikson, *Childhood and Society*, p. 258.
    35. Erikson, *Identity*, p. 220.
    36. *Erikson, Young Man Luther*, pp. 134–35.
    37. Erikson, *Childhood and Society*, p. 406.
    38. Erikson, *Insight and Responsibility*, pp. 92–93.
    39. Cassirer, *The Myth of the State*. See also Wheelis, *The Quest for Identity*, pp. 162–67, 200, on the decline of institutionally oriented super-ego in favor of instrumental values.

lem of continuity challenges the ego throughout life: ". . . fate always combines changes in inner conditions, which are the result of ongoing life stages, and changes in the milieu, the historical situation. Identity connotes the resiliency of maintaining essential patterns in the processes of change." [40]

The characteristics of *resiliency* and *continuity* are crucial to understanding Erikson's view. A human being is no simple machine whose dynamics are unidirectionally channeled. Wolfgang Kohler's extensive research on stimulus-response relationships in perception (summarized in *Gestalt Psychology*) reveals that human knowledge transcends specific stimulus inputs.[41] The relational and organizational patterns an individual generates in the process of knowing may be heavily informed by *sets* of stimuli, but there are no purely topographical mechanics which can explain the perceptual closures which occur. What Kohler observes in studies of perception, Erikson encounters in studies of human response to social stimuli. A human being is tenacious and flexible, though not infinitely so, in striving for coherence amid the promptings of body, conscience, senses, and society. Just as Gestalt psychology documents the central tendency of humans to impose consistency in ambiguous, incomplete, or discontinuous perceptual encounters (and what other kinds are there?), so also does the ego try to jockey reality into a more intelligible, though self-serving, perspective.

Erikson and others have suggested that a crucial axis around which life revolves is the division between introspection and activity. The more complicated and uncertain an environment becomes, the more one is likely to turn inward to a simplifying nonempirical faith. The truly healthy ego is able to match inner resources with meaningful activity.[42] Since politics is a process for regulating change, it is the responsibility of political scientists to

40. Erikson, *Insight and Responsibility*, p. 96.
41. Wolfgang Kohler, *Gestalt Psychology* (New York: New American Library, 1947), Ch. 4, "Dynamics As Opposed to Machine Theory," pp. 60–79.
42. Erikson, "Identity and the Life Cycle," pp. 112–15. See also Edelman, *Politics as Symbolic Action*, pp. 59–60.

elaborate those conditions which will fit the procedures for change to the capacities of human nature.

A number of behavioral studies can be interpreted in this context; Michel Crozier's intensive investigation of French bureaucracy concludes that people behave bureaucratically out of a need for personal security and avoidance of face-to-face relations (with deleterious effects on self-identity), and that the elaboration of bureaucracy can lead to the overtaking of the ends by the means. Progressive rigidification decreases output efficiency and eventually becomes dysfunctional to the personal motives of the participants.[43] Robert Nisbet suggests that contiguous aggregates of people without communal functions (e.g., suburbs) generate alienation and despair.[44] Erikson's thesis is that the continuum between overorganization and anomie can be measured through an understanding of identity functions.

Before attempting a more specific discussion of the politics of identity, we should confront the question of identity as a description of social purpose. Erikson comments,

> In order to create people who will function effectively as the bulk of the people, as energetic leaders, or as useful deviants, even the most "savage" culture must strive for what we vaguely call a "strong ego" in its majority or at least in its dominant minority—*i.e.*, an individual core firm and flexible enough to reconcile the necessary contradictions in any human organization, to integrate individual differences, and above all to emerge from a long and unavoidably fearful infancy with a sense of identity and idea of integrity.[45]

Identity summarizes the principal prerequisite for the survival of people as *human* beings. The best use of social power is to supply the means to this end.

Erikson's ethics invite a reconsideration of the philosopher's concern with the gap between "is" and "ought." Identity is a func-

---

43. Michel Crozier, *The Bureaucratic Phenomenon* (Chicago: University of Chicago Press, 1964), pp. 53–54. See also Verba, *Small Groups and Political Behavior*, p. 173.

44. Nisbet, *Community and Power*, p. xv.

45. Erikson, *Childhood and Society*, pp. 185–86.

tional relationship in human life. Identity cannot be achieved without others. The mutuality of identity, presaged specifically by Mead and analyzed by Erikson, generates a need for certain observances which are the same as an ethics of human behavior. If *in fact* one's purpose is to form a self-identity, and if *in fact* one can't do this without the cooperation of others, does that still add up to saying that I *ought* to treat others according to the ethics of mutual identity formation? Why not simply victimize the others necessary to my identity formation and hang the consequences for them? I may succeed though my neighbors may suffer.

This philosophical box is illusory if we keep in mind the purpose of the argument. The point is to develop a good argument for persuading individuals that they and everyone else will be better off if certain value commitments are made. Erikson's clinical observations on identity formation furnish evidence for that. Second, individuals must be persuaded that certain identities are socially destructive. Once again, relationships of involuntary and permanent dominance can be clinically demonstrated to be repressive to the formation of identity. The third problem gets to the core of the matter: how to persuade individuals that violating social norms for personal advantage is wrong. Again, Erikson can argue from his research that victimization is a psychological death trap for both victor and vanquished. If I make my neighbors suffer, so also will I suffer: "Exploitation exists where a divided function is misused by one of the partners involved in such a way that for the sake of his pseudo aggrandizement he deprives the other partner of whatever sense of identity he had achieved, of whatever integrity he had approached. The loss of mutuality which characterizes such exploitation eventually destroys the common function and the exploiter himself." [46]

What's left? There is still the puzzling word *ought*. The hovering phantom in that term is the idea of an absolute which will give to *ought* a logically defensible imperative mood. "We ought to because God said so," is the prototype of all such arguments. The absoluteness is derived from an absolute (God) and transferred to

46. *Ibid.,* p. 418.

the ethical maxim identified as a command of God. The theologians who assert that there can be no absolutist ethics without God are quite right. It is impossible to bridge the gap between *is* and *ought* in their absolutist sense.

Are those who do not believe in a god then forever condemned to an ethicless existence? I think not. Erikson's arguments, approximations that they are, amount to a persuasive case from empirical evidence that certain consequences will flow from certain activities. The reason the consequences will flow is specified in terms of a quasi-teleological argument about identity. Identity may be an approximation, but I think it more sensible to base an ethics on an empirically defensible approximation which summarizes much accumulated insight into human nature than to base ethics on an abstraction the only philosophical virtue of which is a dubious absolutism. Erikson envisions an evolutionary ethics "not based on the moral injunction of avoiding affront to the ideal but on the ethical capacity to provide strength in the actual." [47] The genius of Gandhi, according to Erikson, was his ability to transform and modify absolutist morality into truth in real action while attending to the behavioral modalities of human beings.[48]

Erikson's argument is somewhere in between an entirely relativist examination of the connection between a specific act "A" and a specific consequence "B," and the absolutist ethics of the religionist. By supplying a process-oriented statement of human purpose, Erikson has moved to the nether limit of pragmatism to formulate conclusions about the natural pattern of life in scientifically sensible terms.[49] Identity is far more precise in its implications

47. Erikson, *Insight and Responsibility*, p. 177.
48. Erikson, *Gandhi's Truth*, esp. pp. 411–13.
49. Erikson, *Insight and Responsibility*, p. 157; cf. p. 206. To speak of a "natural pattern of life" is to invoke the whole tradition of natural law and with it a major thread binding the ages of political philosophy. See also Arnold Brecht's capsule history of natural law ideas in *Political Theory* (Princeton, N.J.: Princeton University Press, 1959), pp. 138–42. In a time of mathematical models and symbolic logic the use of a musty, monkish term like "natural" requires a methodological defense. Arthur Bentley and John Dewey proposed a reconciliation of the natural with the contemporary in 1949 when they argued that "man, inclusive of all his knowings, should

for social behavior than previous process-oriented generalizations such as Freud's *normality,* Mead's *adjustment,* and Skinner's *survival.* It is a valuable formulation not alone for its precision, but also because it captures what is missing in the others: a sense of

be investigated as 'natural' within a natural world; and, secondly, that investigation can, and must, employ sustained observation akin in its standards—though not, of course, in all its techniques—to the direct observation through which science advances" (*Knowing and the Known,* p. 79). They titled this approach, "transactionalism." What we are asked to do is to seek natural probabilities (rather than laws) and to look for them in the systematic study of human behavior. When Erikson advises us to look to childhood, he is suggesting that political philosophy remove itself from atomistic liberalism and tradition-oriented conservatism in order to seek insights about human growth and development in the context of environment and to plot the consistencies and coordinates of psychic as well as physical survival.

Since Erikson's naming of a central process of life is so significant, it is worth testing his formulation against Dewey and Bentley's methodological prescriptions. They would have three conditions met for the "naming" of a phenomenon: "(1) The names are to be based on such observations as are accessible to and attainable by everybody. This condition excludes, as being negligible to knowledge, any report of purported observation which the reporter avows to be radically and exclusively private. (2) The status of observation and the use of reports upon it are to be tentative, postulational, hypothetical. This condition excludes all purported materials and all alleged fixed principles that are offered as providing original and necessary 'foundations' for either the knowings or the knowns. (3) The aim of the observation and naming adopted is to promote further observation and naming which in turn will advance and improve. This condition excludes all namings that are asserted to give, or that claim to be, finished reports on 'reality'" (*ibid.,* pp. 48–49). The first condition goes to the methodology by which the basis for naming is established—a matter for later discussion in connection with the clinic as a source of insight. The second condition is a prescription based on commitments to pragmatism—commitments a clinician must, by all means, share. The third condition tests the naming according to its heuristic value—a condition met when one views the extensive research and commentary Erikson's formulations have stimulated. Finally, the name *identity* for what goes on in people's working-through of their natural promptings and social environment would seem especially apropos in view of Dewey and Bentley's desire that "The talking, the naming [be] . . . oriented to the full organic . . . process rather than to some specialized wording for self, mind, or thinker, at or near, or perhaps even as, a brain" (*ibid.,* p. 147). Identity formation is a name for the process of ego-in-environment (both physical and cultural).

the construction that goes on in life, or, to be bold, the positive aspect of human life effort.

What gives to Erikson's ethics an imperative quality is not a phantom absolute, but rather an empirically based insight. Skinner's analysis of the inescapability of social control gives us a powerful reason for facing up to the responsibility of settling on the best available approximation to human purpose. If the agencies of social control are not operated according to the best available approximation, they will be operated according to some other necessarily less defensible canon. Even if there is a reserve of free will, no individual is exempt from at least some environmental conditioning. The phenomenon of social control must be faced with ethics in hand. It may be that an individual is not entirely a conditioned creature. The argument stated here has no quarrel with such a possibility. This argument does quarrel with basing ethics on human freedom to the exclusion of human conditioning. An ethics of that kind only benefits those who have the leisure and idiosyncrasy to avoid what is common to others—namely, conditioning. Actually, the very fact that we bother with this kind of argument testifies to a faith in the possibility of altering the direction of human conditioning—and that relies on human choice.

Human life is action, it is commitment—there can be no such thing as an utterly passive human being. Societies, too, make commitments. Hitherto, the free society was conceived to be the one which made the least number of commitments to theories of human behavior so as to allow room for the maximum diversity of individual commitment. But every society excludes some kinds of behavior and institutionalizes other kinds. It is at these boundaries that political philosophy must confront the question of the purpose of society.

The rigidity of these boundaries and their restrictiveness must be a matter for the degree to which a useful principle can be scientifically established and made acceptable to the citizenry. Obviously we do not know enough about the identity function to install Erik Erikson as the preceptor of our society so that all boundary questions can be referred to him. I would suggest that we do know enough to reformulate some of the boundaries and the elements of the social reward and punishment system while still allowing plenty of room for other kinds of commitments.

We may be at the point where it is fair to limit commitments which directly threaten a rational social identity structure and process, even though we are not at the point where we can insist that everyone be committed to this type of society on pain of banishment to a mental institution.

To summarize whatever progress has been made toward a theory of liberation, the specifics of policy have to be addressed. We have in Erikson's theory a framework within which such recommendation can intelligibly be made. It is time to see what a politics of identity consists of.

chapter six

A Politics of Identity

The standards for judging the good citizen and the norms of the good state comprise the two central questions of political philosophy. The two cannot be completely separated by any means. The range of individual actions appropriate in a good state vary drastically from those generally authorized in a bad state. Obedience and obligation are quite different questions in a democratic commune and in Nazi Germany.

Psychological theory clarifies some of the limits on prescribing behavior for individuals. There are also some powerful insights into the designs appropriate for political and social institutions. Erik Erikson's formulations make clear the need for a kind of psychological living space for individuals. A programmed existence deprives people of the possibility of achieving what can only be completed internally: an identity built on a sense of competence and integrity. By mapping that living space, Erikson provides a guide to the role of the state, the community, and even the family. He proposes a positive standard for the judgment of social institutions.

The political meaning of his theory rests largely in making explicit what is implied by his clinically based theory. Using Erikson's insights, we can begin to find answers to the problems of liberation. The structure of a theory of liberation may be seen in terms of four categories: the political relationship between individual and community, the connection between identity development and the control of social power, the detailing of a method for realizing the goals of human development, and the specification of policies basic to a truly human community.

Individual and Community

Erikson delineates the significance of cultural supports for personality development; at the same time he specifies some dimensions of mutuality between individual and community. The agenda, then, for a discussion of individual-community relations is: cultural supports, mutuality, and individual choice.

A casual reading of Erikson might lead to conservative conclusions were it not for Erikson's insights on the role of choice in identity formation and the dysfunctionalism of too much order. Erikson remarks,

> only a gradually accruing sense of identity, based on the experience of social health and cultural solidarity at the end of each major childhood crisis, promises that periodical balance in human life which—in integration of the ego states—makes for a sense of humanity. But wherever this sense is lost, wherever integrity yields to despair and disgust, wherever generativity yields to stagnation, intimacy to isolation, and identity to confusion, an array of associated infantile fears are apt to become mobilized: for only an identity safely anchored in the "patrimony" of a cultural identity can produce a workable psychosocial equilibrium.[1]

So people need culture, but not too much: "Our ego is most powerful when it is not burdened with an excessive denial of our

1. Erik Erikson, *Childhood and Society*, 2d ed., rev. (New York: Norton, 1963), p. 412. Erikson discusses some misconceptions of ego identity in a footnote which bears citing: "The concept of ego identity may be misunderstood in two ways. One may suspect that all identity is conformist, that a sense of identity is achieved primarily through the individual's complete surrender to given social roles and through his unconditional adaptation to the demands of social change. No ego, it is true, can develop outside of

drives, but lets us enjoy what we can, refute what we must, and sublimate according to our creativity—always making due allowance for the absolutism of our conscience, which . . . must always remain part of the whole performance." [2] If Erikson said nothing more than that total autonomy and total order are unrealistic alternatives, he could hardly be credited with originality. He offers much more, however, in his intricate analysis of the appropriate mixture of individual initiative and cultural supports.[3]

Two of Erikson's epigenetic stages illustrate the insights generated by his theory. In infancy, the adequacy and responsiveness of supportive functions must meet certain standards in the world of the infant. Failing the achievement of "basic trust," the child is foredoomed to difficulty. Research in the clinic and in small groups bears this out.[4] Similarly, at the other end of the life cycle, Erikson notes a central ambivalence between *integrity* and *despair*. Integrity is a feeling of rightness about one's participation in the cosmos. In a society whose processes make sense in the perspective of old age, the individual who has found an identity and worked it through the crises of life may face death with the assur-

social processes which offer workable prototypes and roles. The healthy and strong individual, however, adapts these roles to the further processes of his ego, thus doing his share in keeping the social process alive. The second misconception concerns those individuals who devote themselves to the study and the lonely pursuit of human integrity and who in doing so seem to live beside and above the group from which they have emerged. Are they above all identity? Such individuals were, in their development, by no means independent of their group's identity, which, in fact, they may have absorbed to the point of outgrowing it. Nor are they free from a new common identity, though they may share it only with a very few who may not even be living in the same era (I am thinking here of Gandhi, and his relationship both to India and to Jesus of Nazareth)" (*ibid.*).

2. Erik Erikson, *Young Man Luther: A Study in Psychoanalysis and History*, p. 216. See also George Homans, *The Human Group* (New York: Harcourt, 1950), esp. p. 272.

3. Erik Erikson, *Identity: Youth and Crisis* (New York: Norton, 1968), p. 224.

4. Erikson, *Insight and Responsibility* (New York: Norton, 1964), p. 231; *Young Man Luther,* p. 118; *Childhood and Society,* pp. 247–50; Sidney Verba, *Small Groups and Political Behavior: A Study of Leadership* (Princeton: Princeton University Press, 1961), p. 40.

ance that life is, after all, meaningful.[5] Each stage between infancy and old age carries its particular demands for a supportive mutual relationship between self and society.

The failure of social mutuality is crippling—the more so the earlier it occurs in the life cycle. Recent research in the social sciences reveals the host of evils for individuals which result from cultural excesses or failures. Sidney Verba relates aggressive behavior to the imposition of excessive external controls on primary group processes.[6] David Apter comments on the paralyzing insecurity of the socially dispossessed.[7] George Homans finds patterns of escapist behavior in socially alienated individuals.[8] To the extent that Erikson correlates specific cultural supports with the epigenetic stages of life, he has increased the utility of his identity concept as a normative standard for a political ethic.

Erikson also furnishes a useful analysis of the dangers of chauvinistic group identifications. Group relatedness does clarify identity: groups provide continuity and structure to the lives of individuals. One potential technique of group identity validation is to idealize one style of life at the expense of others.[9] This is, of course, a theoretical analogy for intergroup aggression. Erikson terms the process of setting up subdivisions of the human race *pseudo-speciation,* as a way of drawing attention to the illusory character of chauvinism, a theme he is presently developing in relation to American history. Regarding the current scene, he comments, "In our era of limitless technological expansion, . . . the question will be what man can afford and decide *not* to use, *not* to invent, and *not* to exploit—and yet save his identity." [10]

5. See Erikson, *Childhood and Society,* pp. 268–69; *Young Man Luther,* pp. 260–61.

6. Verba, *Small Groups and Political Behavior,* pp. 227–28.

7. David Apter, *Ideology and Discontent* (New York: Free Press, 1964), pp. 30–31.

8. Homans, *The Human Group,* pp. 332–33.

9. See Erikson, *Childhood and Society,* pp. 404–5; *Insight and Responsibility,* p. 126; *Identity,* pp. 41–42; *Gandhi's Truth* (New York: Norton, 1969), p. 432; and Apter, *Ideology and Discontent,* p. 29.

10. Erikson, *Insight and Responsibility,* p. 126.

Beyond such renunciations, the goal for our time must be a universalized identity of each individual as a member of the human species. In Mead's terms, the "generalized other" must become humankind as a whole. Erikson's concept of a universalized identity is never clearly defined and therefore could easily be misinterpreted. It may seem to be a recipe for conformism. However, a definition of the concept does emerge from scattered comments which belies that interpretation and gives valuable content to the notion.

In an article bravely entitled "The Golden Rule in the Light of New Insight," Erikson concludes, ". . . the only alternative to armed competition seems to be the effort to *activate in the historical partner what will strengthen him in his historical development even as it strengthens the actor in his own development— toward a common future identity"* (Erikson's italics).[11] His central proposition here as elsewhere is that the common element in human nature consists in a striving for identity based on *competence* and *integrity* in productive, social, and sexual relations. Erikson observes that competence and integrity are more or less objective conditions in the mind, realizable by individuals. It is the attainment of these states of mind that Erikson regards as the Good.[12] Exploitation and totalism may appear as shortcuts to such a condition—and they are ultimately ineffective. What Erikson envisions in the universal identity, I think, is that the social component of one's identity would consist of an appreciation of the potential in all people of achieving an identity based on competence and integrity and a sense of the delicate mutuality upon which that depends. A person dedicated to these understand-

11. *Ibid.*, p. 242; see also *Identity*, pp. 31–32; Erik Erikson and Richard Evans, *Dialogue with Erik Erikson* (New York: Dutton, 1967), p. 110; *Gandhi's Truth*, pp. 266–67, 433; "Identity and the Life Cycle," p. 49. On the role of female identity in universalization, see *Identity*, p. 262. For Erikson's prediction on this matter, see *Insight and Responsibility*, pp. 38–39. On the content of a universal identity, see his comments on the judicious identity in *Childhood and Society*, pp. 416–19.

12. Erikson, *Childhood and Society*, pp. 240, 268–69.

ings and aware that their actualization relies partly on one's own self-realization of inner potential will not be a conformist in the socially damaging sense; rather such a person will be, in the classic phrase, an "enlightened individual."

The enemies of the universal identity are prejudice and intolerance. More specifically, Erikson comments, ". . . the immature origin of his conscience endangers man's maturity and his works: infantile fear accompanies him through life." [13] Thus the strongest supports of the universal identity are cultural arrangements which meet the stages of development in such a way as to overcome the "immature origin of conscience" and shape it into an instrument for judiciousness and openness both to reasonable commitment and future revision.[14]

Erikson may appear to be an environmental determinist. He states that, "anatomy, history, and personality are our combined destiny." [15] But by "personality" he is referring to that complex of choices which the individual makes in creating an identity. Persons make the environment while adapting to it.[16] In his biographical studies of Gandhi and Luther, Erikson shows how both of them creatively resolved personal identity crises with vast effect on the world. When Luther declared "Here I stand," he was demonstrating the power of one individual's choice.[17] Gandhi burst the restraints of environment to forge a new integration of Indian ethical and political identity.[18]

Originality may develop out of idiosyncrasy, but only inhumanity can result from total isolation.[19] Life always proceeds in a web of social relations, but the web must not bind too tightly. Mead's analysis of growth through role-playing established the need for experimental latitude in the life of the child. The possibility of

---

13. *Ibid.*, p. 405.
14. *Ibid.*, p. 416.
15. Erikson, *Identity*, p. 285.
16. Heinz Hartmann, *Essays on Ego Psychology* (New York: International Universities Press, 1964), p. 31.
17. Erikson, *Young Man Luther*, p. 231.
18. Erikson, *Gandhi's Truth*, p. 120.
19. Erikson, *Identity*, p. 249.

choice within and beyond the immediate environment remains crucial to all human life.[20]

The reconciliation of social mutuality and liberation theory is not as difficult as it might appear. *Equality,* the classic value of liberation theory, has always been the most troublesome political value to analyze and justify. Empirical studies of behavior usually reveal inequality to be an objective fact. Efforts to create "objective" physiological or mental characteristics between races as a way of supporting arguments for egalitarian attitudes inevitably run into such absurdities as claiming that length of cranium (or I.Q.) is somehow the crucial determinant of a person's worth. Yet the point of this discussion is to suggest that human beings share a common nature. If it can be inferred that identity achievement is central to all people, then there is a powerful argument for equality as a political value. Without a common minimum of security and opportunity and without basic social tolerance of diverse identities, individual humanness and humanity collectively are endangered.[21] Both victor and vanquished are psychologically damaged in a society which reinforces exploitation.

While exploitation is a danger, so also is a kind of therapeutic leveling. As Philip Rieff comments, "Life is individual. Well-being is a delicate personal achievement, and only a vulgarization of the analytic attitude would permit easy or general judgements on any such achievement." [22] Or Erikson, who puts enforced salvation in a socio-political context: ". . . once we have learned to reduce 'the other'—*any* living human being in the wrong place, the wrong category, or the wrong uniform—to a dirty speck in our moral vision, and potentially a mere target in the sight of our (or our

20. Erikson, "Identity and the Life Cycle," p. 26; Hartmann, *Ego Psychology,* p. 18. On determinism, see *Dialogue with Erik Erikson,* pp. 37–38; *Young Man Luther,* pp. 111–12. By contrast, consider Freud, *The Future of an Illusion,* trans. by W. D. Robson-Scott, rev. and ed. by James Strachey (New York: Anchor, 1964), pp. 7–8. On Konrad Lorenz, see Erikson, *Gandhi's Truth,* pp. 426–27. As for American cultural identity, see *Childhood and Society,* Ch. 8, pp. 285–325.

21. Erikson, *Gandhi's Truth,* p. 244.

22. Philip Rieff, *The Triumph of the Therapeutic* (New York: Harper, 1966), p. 50; see also Erikson, "Identity and the Life Cycle," p. 110.

soldiery's) gun, we are on the way to violating man's essence, if not his very life." [23] As Erikson suggested in the 1972 Godkin Lectures, My Lai is the quintessential case of a confrontation between a chauvinistic identity and the denial of another's humanity on which that identity was built. The massacre was an instance of "a dream that played itself out and a nightmare made real in broad daylight." [24]

Robert Lane raises a troublesome point when he suggests that a *social* emphasis on equality can produce *individual* attitudes which are precisely the reverse. The reason is that individuals who occupy low status positions rationalize their status inferiority by denigrating those even lower in status. This is likely in Erikson's perspective if the culture values status and its accoutrements as an end object. It is similar to the phenomenon he calls *pseudo-speciation*. A natural society oriented to individual self-realization for its own sake would presumably create less pressure to rationalize self in terms of external status. One could argue that it is not the emphasis on equality which bothers Lane's respondents as much as the American cultural emphasis on material measures of status.[25]

The basis for *obligation* in Erikson's theory is mutuality. Both Freud and Mead demonstrated that social relations are intrinsic to any individual's existence. Erikson adds a standard for discrimination in obligation when he specifies the cultural supports necessary to self-realization. One is obligated to respect the lives and inner selves of others because one's own life is dependent on the reflexiveness of social interaction.[26] One is obligated to the state if, on balance, it offers the essentials for self-realization.[27] Self-defense is the test of obligation, only much more is involved

23. Erikson, *Gandhi's Truth*, pp. 390–91. See also *Childhood and Society*, pp. 315–16; *Insight and Responsibility*, p. 233.

24. The Godkin Lectures, sponsored by the John Fitzgerald Kennedy School of Government, were given on April 11 and 12, 1972, at Harvard University. Erikson's statement was quoted in the *Harvard Crimson*, April 13, 1972, p. 6.

25. Lane, *Political Ideology*, pp. 61, 79–80.

26. Erikson, *Insight and Responsibility*, p. 154.

27. Erikson, *Childhood and Society*, p. 254.

than returning the fire of an assailant. Self is partly social, and the defense of the society against a clear threat to its institutions by a society with *self*-destructive institutions is valid. Application to cases must revolve around the classical criteria of the nature and directness of the threat. People's *positive* obligation to the state is to enhance those processes and supportive functions that help individuals to realize themselves.

Erikson's implicit political theory consists of more than values and a theory of obligation, however. In the style of his chart of epigenetic human development, he lists the virtues which must accompany each of the stages. The term *virtue* may seem strange in what is supposed to be an empirically based argument for natural values. Yet Erikson makes a case that the acquisition of specific virtues is functional (and, in this sense, natural) to the development of personality. Erikson's list includes: *"Hope, Will, Purpose,* and *Competence* as the rudiments of virtue developed in childhood; . . . *Fidelity* as the adolescent virtue; and . . . *Love, Care,* and *Wisdom* as the central virtues of adulthood." He goes on to remark, "In all their seeming discontinuity, these qualities depend on each other. Will cannot be trained until hope is secure, nor can love become reciprocal until fidelity has proven reliable." [28] In childhood, for example, the trauma of separation and increasing isolation generate the ego crisis of basic trust, and it is in this battle that hope, will, and purpose become crucial virtues. Similar reactions are indicated for each of the psycho-sexual stages of life.

Are these virtues innate? "Man is born only with the capacity to learn to hope, and then his milieu must offer him a convincing world view and within it specific hopes," writes Erikson.[29] Political science must seek out the forms and styles of government which contribute to the formation of such an environment. If Erikson is right, humankind will be forever unsettled in any environment which does less than support an honest self-realization.[30]

28. Erikson, *Insight and Responsibility,* p. 115.
29. Erikson, *Dialogue with Erik Erikson,* p. 30.
30. Erikson, *Insight and Responsibility,* p. 139.

The correlates of environmental failure are many. An unjust state creates the conditions in which the state itself becomes the object of malevolent projections in the minds of its citizens. When the state does wrong, Erikson suggests, it not only deprives its citizens of essentials, but it also becomes the victim of its own failure through the tendency of individuals to symbolize and mythologize their frustration.[31] The conspiracy myth is the prototype. A socially insecure environment yields a vicious circle of rigidification through impersonal rule procedures.[32] Educational failures commonly generate an appetite for authoritarian social arrangements.[33] It takes no exhaustive review of the literature to bring home to our own life histories the specific behavioral correlates to environmental failure; a little retrospection is sufficient.

Identity and Power

One good test of an innovative theoretical framework for politics is its ability to refresh old insights in a more lifelike approximation to reality. Much of the following discussion about power, planning, and justice involves the familiar; but one hopes the logic will be clearer and the conclusions more usable than in traditional liberal theory.

The one broad class of identities which society has an inherent right to control is that relating to the dominance of one individual by another. Dominance or power is the crucial inter-identity link. Human nature cannot be realized without social structure; and human nature can be destroyed by social structure. Thus we have a right to control, limit, and review exercises of authority.

The task is to form the requisite structures so they operate

31. Erikson, *Childhood and Society*, pp. 377–78, 406.
32. Michel Crozier, *The Bureaucratic Phenomenon* (Chicago: University of Chicago Press, 1964), p. 208.
33. Cited in Verba, *Small Groups and Political Behavior*, from a study by Allen Calvin, Frederic Hoffman, and Edgar Hardin, "The Effect of Intelligence and Social Atmosphere on Group Problem Solving Behavior," *Journal of Social Psychology*, Vol. 45 (1957), pp. 61–74. See *Small Groups*, p. 235.

within the range of human authority tolerance. Anarchism won't work. Freud's partial but powerful etiology of human neurosis shocked the Western intellect into facing the impact of childhood conditioning. Mead found in role-taking, which is essentially a conditioning process, a basic mechanism of evolutionary adaptation. Skinner shows us that social-control functions operate in any event whether or not the state plays a part.[34] And Erikson explores the parameters of individual choice in relation to the shape of one's society. In the face of these realities, we must develop a positive theory of political power.

The control of power vexes every political theorist. The old maxim about power and corruption has been revised: "absolute power corrupts, but the absence of power corrupts abolutely." It doesn't take much psychology to see why. The individual who acquires absolute power has the possibility of working personal designs on others. These designs may well not be coincidental with the welfare of others. Exploitation usually accompanies the attainment of too much power. As the negative results of exploitation feed back into the calculations of the power-holder, corruption sets in. The retention of power regardless of consequences becomes an object in itself.

At the other end of the scale, powerlessness means precisely the inability to control events in one's own life, let alone in the lives of others. To be totally at the mercy of others devastates the individual's capacity to settle with the forces of personal development. At that point, the whole tissue of social mutuality can dissolve. Why play by the rules of the system, when the system is the problem?

One response is the formation of a whole extralegal culture

34. See B. F. Skinner's comment on "dominance" in *Walden Two* (New York: Macmillan, 1948), p. 112. While the attempt here is to suggest bridges between ego psychology and theories of behavioral conditioning, Henry Kariel points out the very profound differences in implications when one or the other is taken as gospel. "The Political Relevance of Behavioral and Existential Psychology," *American Political Science Review*, Vol. LXI, (June 1967), No. 2, pp. 334–42. Cf. Erikson's affirmation of existential psychology in *Dialogue with Erik Erikson*, pp. 88–89.

founded in reaction to conventional society, yet ironically containing many of the same vices in different forms. There is an exaggeration of the goodness of us and the badness of them, a casual attitude toward the symbols and objects by which outgroup people construct their lives, and a cynicism about property which succeeds only in increasing individual insecurity. In the very nadir of powerlessness, some groups find a new kind of power: the power to say "no" to the system. To say "no" to an unjust system is a classic act of protest, but it doesn't solve the problem of what to say "yes" to.

Part of the answer to the harnessing of power for legitimate social ends lies in understanding the nature of the system we now have and how it creates "ins" and "outs." There are two systems of power in this country: economic and political.

The economic system consists of a market where the game generally goes to the swift and the ruthless. Rewards accrue to those who can attach themselves to some enterprise which controls an important service or commodity. Power in the market consists of the ability not so much to serve human needs as to manipulate them for profit. The affliction of unchecked power can be found as easily in large corporations as in large unions, in large educational institutions as in large churches. The agents of each control something people want.

Nothing in the market system itself hinders either monopolistic tendencies or exploitation in the name of competition. The only sufficiently potent source of intervention lies in the political system, to which we will shortly turn. The point is that power is unequally distributed in the economic system. Some have more than others, and they are able to perpetuate their advantages through organization, cunning, and corruption. From positions of power in the market, elites can build and perpetuate economic security for the few at the expense of the many.

The political system, by contrast, is ostensibly organized on a more democratic principle. Each person is supposed to have a vote. It has taken two hundred years for the American system to approximate that formula. While some obstacles to democracy still exist in the form of needlessly complex registration and residency provisions, the era of one person–one vote has arrived. The key to liberation in America has always depended upon mobilizing the political system to control the excesses of the economic system. That revolution can be realized only if the two systems are indeed separated from each other, with preeminence accorded to political decisions.

Clearly that hasn't happened. The political and economic systems are intertwined. The results are everywhere to be seen, from the appointment of regulatory officers from client industries to the use of cash to subvert such democracy as exists in the choice of candidates. Public policy too easily can be purchased not by the vote, but by the dollar.

This situation has been around for a long time, but recent developments have accelerated the trend. Since the Depression, it has become axiomatic that the president is responsible for the state of the economy. If it crashes, so also does he. Senators and representatives experience the same pressures. Congress, recognizing its own hydra-headedness, has delegated ever greater power to the president for the regulation of the economy. A perusal of recent initiatives by the presidency in the area of economic policy reveals that the president can do almost anything he wants to the economy. He can inflate or deflate prices, control the circumstances of production, manipulate the monetary situation, declare freezes and thaws. Recent exercises of this power look haphazard and ineffectual until the corporate profit picture is consulted. While nearly every wage earner has suffered, the government, at least in the short term, has delivered a bonanza to selected corporate clients. No bastion of power in the economy remains secure without an anchor in the government. Small wonder the wry aphorism "Socialism for the rich and free enterprise for the poor" rings so true. We have in fact achieved a form of state socialism without the inconvenience of governmental ownership of the means of production. But the goals of American state socialism remain captive to corporate interests.

How then to keep politics from being dominated by money?

One solution is of course to replace the market with an economy planned at the top. Orthodox socialism formally subordinates economic to political power. It may be we are coming to that. Before the market is completely jettisoned, however, some consideration should be given to the advantages of the market system from a psychological point of view. The market can allow some individuals the chance to be productive and to express themselves in a socially useful manner. By leaving open the possibilities of individual creativity and by allowing some freedom of consumption patterns, the right kind of market can be liberating to the process of human development.

On the other side of equation are the competitive pressures that debilitate human sensitivity and even destroy personality. The individual cost of unrestrained competition may be read in the statistics of alcoholism, divorce, suicide, and "white collar" crime. Then there is the social cost of environmental destruction. A competitive market economy contains no inherent limits on the appropriation of resources until the exhaustion of the resource base forces up prices. The cost to the landscape, to the ecology of the planet, and to the probability of survival itself is extremely high.

The market must be regulated. There must be some way to appropriate a share of its productivity to the provision of basic security for all. There must be some way to place limits on the competitive impulse by altering rewards and penalizing excesses. There must be some way to guarantee the measured use of basic natural resources through central planning.

The specific laws required could be written if there were a power base to legislate and enforce them. The creation of that power base rests on the insulation of the political system from the economic system. While the connections of money and politics at the national level are highly visible, the picture from the congressional district level on down to the local level is one of media oligarchies, wealthy patrons, secretive procedures, and ridiculously complicated jurisdictions. All of this removes accountability from the grasp of the public and places it in the hands of the wealthy and the shrewd. There is no real community here because there is no facing up to the real interests people have in developing competence and integrity. Those at the top can inflict on those at the bottom their priorities, including their recipes for salvation.

Such an increase in public accountability requires a reduction in the role of political money and an increase in the availability of comprehensive information. The public has available few intelligible indicators of community life. In order to get an accurate picture of the social environment, citizens have to work their way through a maze of information generated by self-serving agencies and organizations. Belatedly, important work is being done on "social indicators." We need a Dow Jones index of social disorder, of deprivation, of the successes and failures of social experiments. Certainly, the dangers of sloppy quantifications are very great, but the existing arrangements for transmitting information about the state of the community are worse. We need to build a structure for supplying such information, and the internal controls for reliability, accuracy, and exacting formulation must be very stringent.

Clearly, the social nature of human beings requires a kind of participative planning based on an expanding education of leaders and followers alike. Part of that education involves study of what the self is, but part of it also requires an understanding of both the positive requirements and the self-sacrifices necessary to the institution of planning.[35] The simple awareness of one's personal identity needs without a concomitant knowledge of the social ingredients of the identity-formation process can result in destructive selfishness. Lasswell sums up the meaning of a psychologically liberated democracy: "Our conception of democracy is that of a network of congenial and creative interpersonal relations. Whatever deviates from this pattern is both anti-democratic and destructive." [36] The state cannot be programmed according to an iron logic of therapy without destroying its people's own capacity

35. See Erik Erikson, *Insight and Responsibility*, pp. 209–10.
36. Harold Lasswell, *Power and Personality* (New York: Norton, 1948), p. 110.

for self-development and without channeling their energies into destructive impulses. But the natural state can work if there is a mutual understanding and exploration among its citizens of the balance between authority and liberty necessary to maximum self-development.

To get some idea of the dimensions of the problem posed by political power, it is helpful to review some standard insights into alienation in conjunction with group theory and bargaining as a political method.

Alienation, to the extent that it can be measured, is a useful index of the failure of a political method. Government by experts, the usual proposal of scientifically oriented theorists, yields a particular kind of alienation. There may be, as Theodore Lowi finds in New York City, a gain in instrumental values such as efficiency, but there is a loss of the feeling (and often the reality) of participation and popular control.[37] Melvin Seeman sums up several aspects of the feeling of alienation as normlessness, powerlessness, meaninglessness, and isolation.[38] The political consequences of these feelings are not unidirectional or easily predictable. Observers have noted consequences as varied as embittered romantic disillusionment, apathy, and irrational forms of activism.[39] One apparent solution is the inclusion of more people in the decision-making process. Yet physical inclusiveness engenders ever more complicated procedures.

Liberal theorists have responded to this dilemma by the elaboration of group theory and the idea of bargaining. It is assumed that people will identify with group interests and that they will

37. Theodore Lowi, *At The Pleasure of the Mayor* (New York: Free Press, 1964), p. 217.
38. Melvin Seeman, "On the Meaning of Alienation," *American Sociological Review*, Vol. 24 (1959), esp. pp. 784–89.
39. Judith Shklar, *After Utopia* (Princeton: Princeton University Press, 1957), pp. 151–52. See also Theodore Adorno et al., *The Authoritarian Personality* (New York: Harper, 1950), p. 671; and Wayne Thompson and John Horton, "Political Alienation as a Force in Political Action," *Social Forces*, 38 (1959–60): 190–95.

feel sufficiently efficacious politically if group leaders are perceived to be involved in the bargaining over policy. The underlying proposition is that the most politically relevant fact about a group is its ostensible "interest." This, in turn, presumes that people are rational utility maximizers—and utility is often implicitly assumed to be material.[40]

Psychological theory suggests an alternative assumption: that the relevant political fact about a group is the identity-role supports it creates. Research on the impact of political symbols suggests that a crucial factor in triggering mass reactions is perceptions of threat to group identity-role functions. Substantive gains or losses are viewed mainly in relation to the rewards received by other groups.[41] *People may generally be rational utility-maximizers, but the utility they are maximizing may be more psychological than economic.* This may explain why economic models of behavior are often so disappointing when applied to the data of behavior.

The kind of planning which results from following David Truman's emphasis on the diversity of claims put forward by groups [42] is neatly characterized by Myerson and Banfield in a discussion of Chicago housing politics:

The process by which a housing program for Chicago was formulated resembled somewhat the parlor game in which each player adds a word to a sentence which is passed around the circle of players: the player acts *as if* the words that are handed to him express some intention (*i.e.,* as if the sentence that comes to him were *planned*) and he does his part to sustain the illusion. In playing this game the staff of the Authority was bound by the previous moves. The sentence was already largely formed when it was handed to it;

40. See Anthony Downs, *An Economic Theory of Democracy* (New York: Harper, 1957).

41. Murray Edelman, *The Symbolic Uses of Politics* (Urbana: University of Illinois Press, 1964), Ch. 8, "Persistence and Change in Political Goals," pp. 152–71, and Ch. 9, "Mass Responses to Political Symbols," pp. 172–87.

42. David Truman, *The Governmental Process* (New York: Knopf, 1951), p. 37.

Congress had written the first words, the Public Housing Administration had written the next several, and then the Illinois Legislature, the State Housing Board, the Mayor and City Council, and the CHA Board of Commissioners had each in turn written a few. It was up to the staff to finish the sentence in a way that would seem to be rational, but this may have been an impossibility.[43]

It may be, as Dahl and Lindblom would have it, "The fact of conflicts in goal seeking might be regarded as the fundamental political situation, the basic human condition . . . ," but their recommendation that the process of conflict be institutionalized is not a complete solution.[44] There is a distinction to be made between institutionalizing the forces responsible for conflict and institutionalizing a method for solving problems. Institutionalized conflict is sensible only up to the point where a true identity of interest among diverse parties can be recognized, and then it is time for settlements. As the crises of social policy-making become more frequent, we need to concentrate on enlarging the basis for settlements rather than building vested interests into the system.

The utility of bargaining or any other political method lies in its relation to the ends of the society.[45] Conflict-avoidance is hardly an end in itself—certainly not for liberals—yet there is a tendency to make this the justification for polyarchy. There are certain environmental conditions which are inhuman. Erikson tells us something about psychological death. At the same time, he has illuminated the close connection between means and ends in social action. The problem facing society is not so much how to avoid conflict as how to get people to face the reality of human nature and agree to the measures necessary to its full development.

Theodore Lowi in *The End of Liberalism* suggests that part of

43. Martin Myerson and Edward Banfield, *Politics, Planning, and the Public Interest* (New York: Free Press, 1955), p. 269.

44. Robert Dahl and Charles Lindblom, *Politics, Economics, and Welfare* (New York: Harper, 1953), p. 33.

45. Gunnar Myrdal, *Value and Social Theory* (New York: Harper, 1958), p. 49.

the answer lies in carrying the politics of "input" to the point of specifying the form and administration of the "output." He would like to see the bargaining concentrated in the rule-making stage rather than being split into one more or less representative process for rule-making and one privileged process for rule-application.[46] He hopes that this will improve the efficiency of translation of the will of the people. Perhaps it would; though the relevant balance is between the need for flexible and intelligent application of the laws on the one hand, and the preservation of the intent of the law on the other. It is doubtful that by systematically rigidifying the rule application process there will result a decrease in alienation or an increase in the public's sense of efficacy.

What basically troubles Lowi is that liberal governments cannot hoist justice above the mark of group politics for lack of a general principle or moral rule. He proposes to legislate such rules by the usual processes and to attend to their impartial enforcement.[47] The argument is circular unless there is agreement on a common logic and a set of values to aim for. Lowi's suggestions for tinkering with the process to reduce the role of privilege and increase the responsiveness of policy administrators are all to the good. He is close to the mark when he says, "Nineteenth-century liberalism was standards without plans. . . . But twentieth-century liberalism turned out to be plans without standards." [48] People need to participate in uncovering the essential standards for policy, and the business of liberation theory is to predispose people to inquiry and action guided by a sound theory of human development. To some extent, the more liberals tell people they are what their immediate material self-interest says they are, the more they will act that way. To adopt a benign posture of neutrality in the bargaining between groups is not liberal, it is conservative. Liberalism should be about liberation, and liberation will not come from

46. Theodore Lowi, *The End of Liberalism* (New York: Norton, 1969), pp. 292–305.
47. *Ibid.,* pp. 289–90.
48. *Ibid.,* p. 288.

condoning the bargaining advantages of privileged groups. The very concept of liberation commits one to the idea that there is something in people's nature which has not yet been set free.

A Political Method

There exists no shortage of laudable goals for politics in this or in most works of political theory. What remains puzzling is the method by which worthy goals can be achieved. The essence of a method—and of the preceding dialectics about participation and planning—may be seen in Gandhi's *satyagraha* or "truth-force." Erikson isolates the meaning of Gandhi's famous doctrine in the relationship between morality and action. Had Gandhi's technique been nothing more than purely moralistic absolutism without regard for the characteristics of his followers (*and* his adversaries), he would have failed. Gandhi's genius was in his realization that moral truth is not an abstraction, it is something which emerges in the process of concerted, carefully informed human action. Under the right conditions (and some of them are known), truth works itself out in the *actuality* of one's confrontation with the inner self and with others. One way to understand the meaning and implications of this method is to examine it in relation to some distinctions between reality and actuality, fact and value.

Erikson comments, "In my clinical ruminations I have found it necessary to split what we mean by 'real' into that which can be known because it is demonstrably correct (factual reality) and that which feels effectively true in action (actuality)." [49] This is a vital distinction. David Easton comments that "A fact is a particular ordering of reality in terms of a theoretical interest." [50] This comes close to saying that there are no facts without values. If the literature on the fact-value distinction demonstrates anything, it is that there is a considerable reluctance to resolve one into the other or, on the other hand, to separate the two completely. In a world

49. Erikson, *Gandhi's Truth*, p. 396. See also Philip Rieff, *Freud: The Mind of the Moralist* (Garden City, N.Y.: Anchor, 1961), pp. 333–36.
50. David Easton, *The Political System* (New York: Knopf, 1953), p. 53.

of imperfect knowledge perceived by limited creatures, perhaps the best that can be done is to admit two modes of reality. Erikson's "factual reality" is never quite free of subjectivity, nor is his "actuality" entirely divorced from appreciation of the facts. Notice that Erikson ties "actuality" to that which is "effectively true in action" —thus he imposes an empirical, pragmatic test as a governor of clinical reality. Furthermore, it is a test which involves both parties to the encounter. There is a meeting of the clinician with an informed view of mental disorders and the patient with an informed view of a personal history. The cure is effected not by the clinician pigeonholing the patient in some objective category of illness—that is only a preliminary diagnostic tool—but rather by a matching of *potentialities:* the clinician's capacity for effective insight and the patient's internal strength and capabilities. The sum of this encounter, the cure, goes beyond a reliance on factual reality through an invocation of human potential.

In light of this analysis of the clinical encounter, the distinction between facts and values, one objective and the other emotional, seems somehow to be shallow and incomplete.[51] What accounts in our argument for such a judgment is the proposition, and it is basic to a natural view, that there is something more to human reality than the apparent surface phenomena of the present. In a sense, a human being is a continuous animal in that his or her present is inextricably tied to perceptions of past and future, appearance and potential. There is no radical cleavage between the phenomenal and the spiritual world, as nineteenth-century German thought proclaimed, but neither can one be resolved usefully in terms of the other.[52] Nor is there any radical cleavage between the knower and the known. All we have to go on are shared meanings which are more or less functional to the manipulation of reality in the fulfillment of human needs.[53]

Psychoanalysis is a model of *satyagraha.* Comparing Freud's psy-

51. *Ibid.,* pp. 221–31.
52. H. Stuart Hughes, *Consciousness and Society* (New York: Knopf, 1958), p. 186.
53. Dewey and Bentley, *Knowing and the Known,* p. 80.

choanalytic method and Gandhi's nonviolent confrontations, Erikson concludes, ". . . in both encounters only the militant probing of a vital issue by a nonviolent confrontation can bring to light what insight is ready on both sides." [54] There is a kind of truth in humankind, Erikson is saying, and it comes out in the context of action.[55]

54. Erikson, *Gandhi's Truth,* p. 439, cf. pp. 427–28, 438. Erikson has some specific advice for protesters drawn from his analysis of Gandhi's experiences: "As to the rules for the resisters, they must *rely on themselves,* for both their suffering and their triumph must be their own; for this reason Gandhiji forbade his striking workers to accept outside support. The movement must *keep the initiative,* which includes the willingness to atone for miscalculations as well as the readiness to adapt to changes in the opponent, and to readjust both the strategy and (as far as they were negotiable) the goals of the campaign. And in all of this, the resister must be consistently *willing to persuade* and to enlighten, even as he remains ready *to be persuaded* and enlightened. He will, then, not insist on obsolete precedent or rigid principle, but will be guided by what under changing conditions will continue or come to feel true to him and his comrades, that is, will become *truer through action.*" *Ibid.,* pp. 415–16.

55. It is interesting that the Golden Rule involves a test for the rightness of action which is behavioral rather than mystical or, at the other pole, objectively scientific. "Do to no one what you would not want done to you." This bit of wisdom from another age, it is reasonable to suggest, finds acceptance by a broad spectrum of otherwise differing peoples because it incorporates people's experience into their morality. The *lex talionis* was overthrown in the New Testament on the premise that depriving social relations of violence and exploitation would open the way for the emergence of a higher truth (*The Jerusalem Bible,* ed. Alexander Jones, New York: Doubleday, 1966; see also Tobit 4:15, Matthew 7:12, Luke 6:31, Matthew 5:38–48). Aristotle declares in *The Politics* that "Goodness by itself is not enough: there must also be a capacity for being active in doing good" (Barker translation, New York: Oxford University Press, 1962, p. 289). The meaning is apparent in the *Nicomachean Ethics* when Aristotle relates justice to proportion in human action and notes the ability of good men (those who abide by his rule) to achieve unanimity while those who do bad are inevitably divided (W. D. Ross edition, London: Oxford University Press, 1915, 1131b–37b, 1167b).

There is truth to be found in the confrontation with others and with the environment through reasoned inquiry. Arnold Brecht observes, "Whenever we have been convinced by truth we cannot escape following its signposts in our transtraditional ideas of justice. When we come to see that our convictions or beliefs were based on erroneous assumptions concerning facts, or on poor thinking, they may gradually break down and change; and

The common elements linking together these insights are truth, which emerges from self-disciplined nonviolent encounters, and with truth, justice. Violence complicates any encounter because it creates victors and victims whose disposition to truth and to justice is distorted by emotional responses.

All of this sounds good, but how does a society come to be guided by truth-force? How do people persuade themselves to rely on reality testing (or actuality testing) rather than exaggerated symbols and myths? Edelman's research into the uses of symbol and myth indicates that under conditions of ambiguity and uncertainty, real or induced, about one's material and psychological survival, there is a sharply increased tendency to latch on to simplifying explanations and to avoid reality testing.[56] The cure for this is in part political and economic. A society which allocates whatever it can to overcoming basic scarcities of material goods also creates the conditions for individual "knowing" most likely to engender a rational and natural approach to life. However, *the scarcity is twofold—it is psychological as well as material and the two are inextricably linked.* Neither a society of well-fed slaves nor a society of psychologically liberated paupers have overcome the kind of uncertainty or ambiguity which lead away from reality testing and its social dividend: truth-force.

Thus, policy about the distribution of rewards and processes for

when they do so, even if we try to conceal it, our transtraditional ideas and feelings of justice will change apace. We cannot help it. Science, in fighting for truth, simultaneously remodels evaluations, *and along with them the ideas and feelings of justice" (Political Theory,* Princeton, N.J.: Princeton University Press, 1959, p. 413).

56. Murray Edelman, *Politics as Symbolic Action: Mass Arousal and Quiescence* (Chicago: Markham, 1971), pp. 54–56. The author stresses the point that "deprivation is universal; beliefs about it and adjustments to it are socially cued." The overcoming of basic scarcities is obviously a step in the right direction, but it must be seen in the context of the measures to be discussed later for dealing with the psychological dimensions of scarcity. "Knowings are behaviors," as Bentley and Dewey suggest (though in a different context—*Knowing and the Known,* p. 74), and it is most important to see that establishing the conditions for individual knowing through reality-testing is crucial to a free and natural society.

the equitable involvement of citizens must be linked in our under-standing as they are in our political natures.

Society needs to enhance political processes which provide non-violent confrontations in which there are mutual commitments to finding solutions. The ballot box can be a focal point for one such confrontation, but only if the channels of communication and in-quiry are open to the exploration of issues and policies. Legisla-tures need to face the task of inquiry rather than to relapse into competitive logrolling. Executives have a responsibility to exercise their power in conjunction with a continuous dialogue on the meaning of their mandate. The courts have an obligation to sum-marize the truth of a society and apply it to residual conceptions and recalcitrant parties to exploitation. Organized social groups must go beyond concretizing short-run or lowest-common-denom-inator formulations of their "interests" in search of an evolutionary development of member's interests and potentialities.

Policies for Liberation

The ultimate assumption of Erikson's view is that human beings, at root, share a common nature and a common interest in mutual self-development. The very nature of that goal means that there are maximum opportunities for exploitative self-seeking, though it also means that self-seeking is eventually self-destructive. *Hu-manity has some control over its own evolution and the business of politics is to liberate our evolutionary potential. The final object of that potential is partly to be found in Erikson's concept of a uni-versal identity based on personal integrity and competence as well as social tolerance. That can only be arrived at through participa-tive processes of social action aimed at collective liberation*

To be more specific, the politics of the natural society must con-centrate on certain issues. Policy directions can be defined on pop-ulation, poverty, social exploitation, minorities, and community formation. There must be no argument about the necessity to con-centrate the major share of society's wealth and ingenuity on the provision of appropriate circumstances for the rearing of children. As Erikson remarks, the goal must be a "joint guarantee to each child of a chance for . . . development." [57] What that goal implies for a population policy needs to be considered in view of the effects of insecurity on the ability of nations to solve the problems of planning and resource distribution.

The basic consideration for population policy must be the ability of the society to provide each individual with a floor of security throughout life. Subsistence is not an adequate term. Society must support a basic existence, not a *sub*-sistence. The necessary material elements are essential as well as the psychological supports which can place individuals on the track to their own self-realization. To create a negative identity for the impoverished and to reinforce it through harassment and vilification is the surest guarantee that, following Skinner as well as Erikson, individuals will be incapacitated from getting together those inner resources which alone strengthen a positive identity.[58] On the global level, the enormous problems of resource distribution will never even be approached so long as insecurity governs the lives of the temporarily rich as well as the permanently poor. Insecurity is a root cause of irrational action and its legacy, exploitation.

Erikson has given us some badly needed specific content for the term exploitation. The cause of social and economic exploitation is essentially a willingness by some to appeal to mistrust, shame, guilt, inferiority, confusion, isolation, stagnation, and despair rather than trust, autonomy, initative, industry, identity, intimacy, generativity, and integrity. Exploitation involves an appeal to weakness rather than strength. The state must encourage those forms and modes of education which lead away from reliance on exploitation of the self as a way of life.[59] Surely, by this standard, American television with its mass retailing of violence and ag-

57. Erikson, *Insight and Responsibility*, p. 132.
58. *Ibid.*, p. 133; *Childhood and Society*, p. 253.
59. See Robert Coles, *Erik H. Erikson: The Growth of His Work* (Boston: Little, Brown, 1970), p. 254.

gressive behavior is a scandal which threatens our very civilization.

A major problem for the natural society is the intricate question of identity development in minorities. There is a paradox in Erikson's writing involving his observations on the impact of destroying indigenous groupings, such as the Indians, and his pleas for a universal identity. But the paradox is really a dialectic. Identity formation is essentially a way of dealing with uncertainty and ambiguity. Unless people are given strength from some source of cultural support, they will never be able to rise above its parochialities to a universalist identity. To socially sanction negative identities for blacks and other minorities through legally enforced discrimination is to invite the confirmation of those identities in adult destructiveness. But to emphasize *mutual* tolerance of indigenous group identities is to create the sources for a strength of character crucial to a "nonviolent confrontation" which can "bring to light what insight is ready on both sides." [60] One of the truisms of the literature on blacks is that integration was too often whiteification. Really human integration can only come after a mutual respect for diverse identities. This may be the solution, but the peril is great. The perversion of group-relatedness into aggressive pseudo-speciation is seemingly at least as easy as the selective reinforcement of those aspects of group identity which are productive. The present evolutionary test of humankind is whether, having isolated this problem, we can solve it.

The style of a natural culture must be in the communities of human relatedness it creates. The isolated provision of minimum specific needs must give way to community-oriented, integrated programs of basic services for the disadvantaged. The mentality that believes human nature to be categorized into four, nine, or fifteen dimensions, each to be aided by a specific, but unrelated, program, is dysfunctional.

Coordinated programs for the administration of minimum needs are one part of a larger conception of community. All the forms of human relatedness must be brought together in communities:

60. Erikson, *Gandhi's Truth*, p. 439.

social services, places of employment, recreation, aesthetic expression, housing, and certain aspects of governmental functions. Taxation and the basic design of national minimums must largely be done at the highest level of government. But the community, for the sake of its own vitality, needs to control as many functions as can carry the community beyond those minimums.[61] Political science has a major role in determining that delicate mix of communal control and national or international guidance which will yield the best prospects for cultural support and the universalization of identity through communal activity.

Conclusion

Three concluding themes require brief treatment: the proximate nature of Erikson's identity concept; his clinical method in the perspective of social science; and the integrative aspects of his thought.

Erikson commented in 1956 that ". . . man, in order to be able to interact efficiently with other human beings and especially so if he wishes to cure and to teach, must at intervals make a total orientation out of a given stage of partial knowledge." [62] While this may be true for individuals, Erikson is the first to admit that the identity concept is not final or fixed as a scientific formulation. It is not even a particularly precise concept:

> At one time, then, it will appear to refer to a conscious *sense of individual identity;* at another to an unconscious striving for a *continuity of personal character;* at a third, as a criterion for the silent doings of *ego synthesis;* and finally, as a maintenance of an inner *solidarity* with a group's ideals and identity. In some respects the term will appear to be colloquial and naive; in another, vaguely related to existing concepts in psychoanalysis and sociology. If, after an attempt at clarifying this relation, the term itself still retains

61. See Verba's discussion of size as a limit on participation (and thus mutuality) in *Small Groups and Political Behavior,* pp. 36–37. See also Erich Kahler, *The Tower and the Abyss* (New York: Braziller, 1957), p. 227.
62. Erikson, *Identity,* p. 226.

some ambiguity, it will, so I hope, nevertheless have helped to delineate a significant problem, and a necessary point of view.[63]

I think the "necessary point of view" (the basic "knowing") evidenced by Erikson's research is the interrelation of self-development with human mutuality and the ethic thus implied. As for the specifics of the identity crisis (in the narrow clinical sense) as *the* problem of our time, it may well be a passing phase in our history, just as Freud's preoccupation with sexual repression is now considered to be dated.[64]

Stephen Toulmin points out that "Science is not an intellectual computing machine; it is a slice of life." [65] The part of life experience of central concern to political theorists must be the relation between individual and community. Another historian of science, Thomas Kuhn, suggests that the choice of an explanatory theory, in a world of imperfect theories, always involves the question: "Which problems is it more significant to have solved?" [66] The proper test of Erikson's identity theory is not whether it explains everything, but whether it explains vital features of the problem of individual and community.

The choice of method always influences the conclusions reached, and this is certainly true of the clinical method. As Erikson remarks, ". . . our subjects want to become whole; and the clinician must have some theories and methods which offer the patient a whole world to be whole in." [67] Yet we have been able to correlate some of Erikson's major findings with those of significant experiments and observations by social scientists, including Lane, Verba, Apter, Converse, Edelman, Festinger, Homans, Crozier, and others. According to Eugene Meehan, ". . . an explanation is defined as a way of organizing human experience to show how or why events occur by linking those events to other events according to

63. Erikson, "Identity and the Life Cycle," p. 102.
64. Erikson, *Gandhi's Truth,* p. 242.
65. Stephen Toulmin, *Foresight and Understanding,* 1st ed. (New York: Harper, 1961), p. 99.
66. Thomas Kuhn, *The Structure of Scientific Revolutions* (Chicago: University of Chicago Press, 1962), p. 110.
67. Erikson, *Insight and Responsibility,* pp. 136–37.

stipulated rules." [68] The clinical method may not be as satisfactory as the experimental method in terms of methodological rigor, but if it meets Meehan's test in producing an explanation, we would be foolish to reject Erikson's theory on methodological grounds. The number of subjects studied in the clinic may be small (though Erikson has studied diverse communities and individuals of all kinds), but it is a very potent sample given the kind of total confrontation his research involves. Where else, in fact, are we likely to find as complete a social scientific transaction as in the clinic? In the last analysis, the theorist, having marshaled inevitably insufficient evidence, must make a leap of commitment to conclusions if action is to be recommended.

Identity is a description of that mental device which directs people's adaptation to environment and their creation of environment. Yet it is an open-ended formulation derived from empirical research. It is also an inherently relational concept, just as health and rationality are relative. [69] There is no such thing as an absolutely identified human being—no Sartrean in-itself-for-itself. [70] The utility of the identity concept is that it indicates some of the reactions and overreactions in people's individual and collective evolutionary development. It also tries to sketch the essential continuum of relativity in human life: the individual's well-being. [71] As Heinz Hartmann comments, ". . . evolution leads to an increased independence of the organism from its environment, so that reactions which originally occurred in relation to the external world are increasingly displaced into the interior of the organism.

68. Eugene Meehan, *Explanation in Social Science* (Homewood, Ill.: Dorsey, 1968), p. 24. See also Meehan, *The Theory and Method of Political Analysis* (Homewood, Ill.: Dorsey, 1965), pp. 228–55.

69. Erikson, *Gandhi's Truth*, pp. 241–42.

70. Jean-Paul Sartre, *Being and Nothingness* (New York: Washington Square Press, 1966), p. 582. Albert Camus bases rebellion on the finding of an abstract identity: "Awareness, no matter how confused it may be, develops from every act of rebellion: the sudden, dazzling perception that there is something in man with which he can identify himself, even if only for a moment." *The Rebel* (New York: Random House, 1956), p. 14. See also Kahler, *The Tower and the Abyss*, p. 252.

71. Erikson, *Insight and Responsibility*, pp. 150–51.

The development of thinking, of the super-ego, of the mastery of internal danger before it becomes external . . . are examples of this process of internalization." [72] Perhaps Erikson has made clear that pseudo-speciation is the next danger to which we must adapt by internalizing a universalized identity, unless humanity is to find itself on the path of the dinosaur.

The problem is not as Freud thought it was. Civilization is not the enemy of the individual; the real enemy is the perversion of individuals and civilizations alike through ignorance of the natural relation between them.[73] Politics has a great deal to do with encouraging or frustrating the conditions in which that ignorance can be overcome by individuals as well as by decision-makers.

The end we must seek is a natural life for all in a natural community. While the history of liberal ideas has been our philosophic foil, it may be that we have been talking of the end of liberalism (and possibly "isms" in general) and envisioning, in its place, the rise of the natural person at home in an authentically human community.

72. Heinz Hartmann, *Ego Psychology and the Problem of Adaptation* (New York: International Universities Press, 1958), pp. 40–41.

73. Norman Brown summarizes Freud's ambiguities on this question: "Freud's writings, taken as a whole, vacillate between two opposite answers to this perpetual question of unhappy humanity. Sometimes the counsel is instinctual renunciation: grow up and give up your infantile dreams of pleasure, recognize reality for what it is. And sometimes the counsel is instinctual liberation: change this harsh reality so that you may recover lost sources of pleasure. And, sometimes, of course, Freud attempts a compromise between the two attitudes. Thus for example the reality-principle, which he first defined nakedly as an allegiance to 'that which is real, even if it should be unpleasant,' is later softened into that 'which at bottom also seeks pleasure—although a delayed and diminished pleasure, one which is assured by its realization of fact, its relation to reality.' This dilemma explains Freud's drift to pessimism." *Life against Death* (New York: Vintage, 1959), p. 57. See also Freud, *Civilization and Its Discontents,* ed. and trans. by James Strachey (New York: Norton, 1961), p. 92.

index